Wildish Things

Wildish Things

An Anthology of New Irish Women's Writing

Edited by
Ailbhe Smyth

ATTIC PRESS

First published in 1989 by
Attic Press
44 East Essex Street
Dublin 2
Ireland

Second impression 1990

British Library Cataloguing in Publication Data
Wildish Things: an anthology of new Irish women's writings
1. English literature. Irish writers, 1945 - Anthologies
2. Irish literature - Anthologies
I. Smyth, Ailbhe
820.8'09415

ISBN 0-946211-74-4 hb
ISBN 0-946211-73-6 pb

Cover Design: Paula Nolan
Typesetting: Phototype-Set Ltd, Dublin
Printing: The Guernsey Press Company Ltd

This book is published with the assistance of the Arts Council/An Chomhairle Ealaíon, Ireland and the Arts Council of northern Ireland.

*... wildish things these
little newbreed Irish girls scarce
parented, not to be grooved into
rectangular requisite ...*

Eithne Strong *Identity*

For women writers everywhere.

AILBHE SMYTH was born and grew up in Ireland. She graduated from University College Dublin where she lectures in French and Women's Studies. She is a founding member of UCD Women's Studies Forum and is currently involved in setting up a Women's Studies programme. Author of *Women's Rights in Ireland* (1984), *Irish Women Academics* (1985) and editor of *Feminism in Ireland* (1988), her articles on feminist politics, theory and culture have appeared in Irish and international magazines and journals. She has one daughter, Lydia, lives in Dublin and believes passionately in the liberating power of women's creativity.

Acknowledgements

To all those who helped in the compilation of this anthology in so many different ways, I offer my warmest thanks. I am especially grateful to Eithne Strong for allowing a phrase from her poem 'Identity' to be used as the title of this collection; to Máirín Ní Dhonnchadha for her work on translations from the Irish; to Deirdre Davitt of Bord na Gaeilge for practical and prompt assistance; to both An Chomhairle Ealaíon/The Arts Council and The Arts Council of northern Ireland for their vital financial assistance; to everyone in Attic Press for their constant encouragement, enthusiasm and expertise.

The editor and publishers gratefully acknowledge permission to reproduce material in this anthology as follows: MARY BECKETT: 'Heaven', © Mary Beckett, 1989. SARA BERKELEY: 'Convalescent' from *Home Movie Nights*, published by Raven Arts Press, Dublin, 1989. EAVAN BOLAND: 'The Shadow Doll', previously published in *The Yale Review*, 1987. DEIRDRE BRENNAN: 'An Tobar', 'Dealbhóireacht', 'Scothanna Geala' from *Scothanna Geala*, published by Coiscéim, Dublin, 1989. MARY DORCEY: 'The Husband' from *A Noise From The Woodshed*, published by Onlywomen Press Ltd., London 1989, © Mary Dorcey and Onlywomen Press. RITA ANN HIGGINS: 'Witch in the Bushes', 'Woman's Inhumanity to Woman', 'Some People' from *Witch in the Bushes* published by Salmon Publishing, Galway, 1988. MÁIRE MHAC an tSAOI: 'Tarlachaint', previously published in *The Irish Times*; 'Cearca', 'I Leith na Ruaidhe', previously published in *Comhar*, September, 1988. FRANCES MOLLOY: 'Women are the Scourge of the Earth' © Frances Molloy, 1989. ÁINE NÍ GHLINN: 'Ospidéal', 'Gairdín Pharthais', 'Coilltiú' from *Gairdín Pharthais agus dánta eile*, published by Coiscéim, Dublin, 1988. MARY E O'DONNELL: 'Reading The Sunflowers in September', previously published in *Oxford Poetry*, November, 1988. EITHNE STRONG: 'An Féar nach Stopfaidh', Coiscéim, Dublin, 1989; 'Yellow Joke' previously published in *Orbis International Poetry Magazine*, 1986.

Contents

Introduction

As I worked on this anthology, a half-remembered legend from Irish mythology pulled at the corners of my consciousness, imprecise but persistent. Reluctantly, I allowed it to surface and understood both its power to disturb and my resistance to it. The legend recounts the fate of a woman who dared to look into the depths of a forbidden well. The water surged up and drowned her, at the same time giving birth to a stream that fructified the country.

The metaphor is powerful and crystal clear. The prohibition against women's quest for creative expression is absolute, the sanction against those who disobey is swift and total annihilation. Women's experiences, visions, voices are fated to be submerged by the relentless flow of patriarchal myth and history, of politics and economics. At our risk and peril do we claim the right to autonomy and imagination.

But what is freedom if we cannot imagine ourselves free? And what is imagination if we may never look into our wildest depths?

Irish women have been bound by negative imperatives for a long time. In this we are surely no different from countless other women elsewhere. And yet, how women confront and ultimately refuse the strictures imposed upon us is not simply an individual matter. Our sense of ourselves, and of our possibilities, is marked by both the larger patterns and the particular details of race, class and nationality, history and culture. The very ways in which we strive to float free of the particular are shaped and moulded by it.

> '..............And the murked cloud
> that presses into the mountain's thighs,
> and the stark brown tree,
> will answer nothing for that woman
> with her wounded hunch of shoulder.'
> (Mary E O'Donnell)

7

That woman and 'the nameless presence that bows her head' is both the same and significantly different across time and place.

For Irish women, the anonymity of womanhood has long been overshadowed by the otherness of Ireland, the difficulty of naming ourselves as women complicated by a national history of colonisation, deprivation and strife, 'sub-melody, sonic undertow' of our lives *(Paula Meehan)*. We are marked ineradicably, in Eavan Boland's phrase, by 'the power of nationhood to edit the realities of womanhood'. Nationality is not, of course, the only sign of identity, but where the struggle to achieve it has been bitter and hard-fought, it cannot be assumed, never goes without saying. The hard fact for Irish women is that our voices have been overwhelmed as much by the needs of the nation as by the dictates of patriarchy. And there is nothing to be gained by denying this, whatever we might prefer to believe. Chrissie, in Evelyn Conlon's story 'On The Inside Of Cars', berates herself with admirable, and unusual, honesty:

> 'Jesus, Chrissie, where are your political morals?
> Just for comfort. Facts were such hard things.
> They could not be changed. Not even the frills of them
> could be turned about to make it easier.'

And it is not easy to write yourself up from under the closely meshed layers of the facts of femininity and Irishness. A woman in Irish literature, at least since the 18th century, is rarely attributed an independent existence. 'The identity of 'woman' with a territory claimed by a masculine power is still deeply engrained' *(Gerardine Meaney)*. 'Woman' serves merely as sub-text, pretext to an idea:

> 'Nuair a d'éirigh sí an mhaidin úd
> ba chrann í is ní nárbh ionadh'
> (When she awoke that morning
> she had turned to tree and it was no surprise)
> *(Áine Ní Ghlinn)*

To know and name our own multiple and diverse realities we must first fight free of the one-dimensional metaphor we have been forced to become. To tell our stories, we must write over the images and myths which overshadow us.

'No one has a job in Kilenarden
nowadays they say it is a no-go area
I wonder, then, who goes and does not go
in this strange forgotten world
of video and valium'
(Leland Bardwell)

Accurate reflection of daily lived lives. Senselessness the only defence against poverty, unemployment, emigration, violence, censorship. Divorce no, abortion no, a job no, no-go, no. Head down, feet together, mouth shut and whatever you say, say nothing.

As women, we have been denied the right to speak by the patriarchs who have appropriated unto themselves exclusive rights of public utterance. Let the sceptics count our voices in the courts, the legislature, the church, the multi-national corporations. And let them also count the anthologies in which women's writings are represented. It will be quickly done.

As Irish, our language has been devalued and marginalised by the colonisers from a culture which has always sought by various means to appropriate Ireland and the Irish.

As Irish women, we are thus doubly damned, doubly silenced. Caught uneasily, awkwardly between our experiences which have no language of their own, a rhetoric which would turn us into metaphor and the terrible magnetic pull towards the hegemonic maelstrom of English and Englishness:

'The very word, small and plain as it is, rolled around my mouth, smooth as ivory. What a deliciously English word it is: Bath. The *a* is a test, the *th* the trial that tells the sheep from the goats, the cultured from the masses, the old from the nouveau and, let me admit it, the English from us.'

(Éilís Ní Dhuibhne)

What language can we speak but that of the oppressor, in whatever guise he comes?

"A man is a man
and a real man
must spit feathers
when the occasion arises."
(Rita Ann Higgins)

Is it so surprising to find a concern with language, and specifically with voice, surfacing with such poignant force in the writings of Irish women? Thematically, symbolically, formally, voice is centrally important. We who have been drowned in 'dull quiet', can we talk? 'Voices - whose voices?' *(Una Woods)*. We who have been belittled by their words, bewildered by their poems, 'Jess wished in a way that he had put her name on a better one. A more grown-up one than this kind of fairy tale about farmers' wives and chickens' *(Maeve Binchy)*. We who have been hurt by the patriarch whose 'words cut much deeper than his hard black shoe' *(Rita Kelly)*. We who have even sought refuge in the 'great sweetness' of a soundless heaven *(Mary Beckett)*. We who dream of a 'Word made genderless' *(Mary E O'Donnell)*. We who question the meaning of their words:

> 'Up there on the platform a man
> speaks of the people: of what
> we need, of who we really are, of how
> we must fight to liberate ourselves.'
> *(Paula Meehan)*

We who must refute centuries of censorship before we can speak of our pleasure and our pain:

> 'Tá oighear á sheideadh
> trí phóirsí fada gaofaire
> sa phabhailiún
> is íochtaraí i mo lár
> Tá na seolphíobáin mothála
> reoite ina stangadh...........'
> (An icy wind blows
> through the cold porches
> of the farthest pavilions
> in the depths of my soul.
> The conduits of emotion
> are all frozen solid........)
> *(Nuala Ní Dhomhnaill)*

Can abortion be spoken of only 'East of Ireland' *(Dolores Walsh)*? Mary Dorcey writing of lesbian sexuality, a rare voice from a deeply hidden pool. Frances Molloy, Maeve Kelly, Rita

Kelly and so many others, speaking the verbal and physical violence done to women. So much still to be said. And when will those voices be heard? 'Every woman is an outlaw, guarding her secrets. Mumbling her riddles at your strong walls' *(Linda Anderson)*. Nuala Ni Dhomhaill writing in Irish which she calls 'the language of the mothers', reinventing for us now an inheritance of myth, folklore and oral tradition which predates the power and prestige accorded to the (male) written word. Biddy Jenkinson refusing the imperialism of translation into English - there are other languages. Eithne Strong in this collection, others elsewhere, moving from one language to the other, although never imperceptibly, consciously seeking a language.

The turn and tone of a voice, an inflection, the most fleeting intonation giving shape to an entire narrative, prose or poem. Monologue, dialogue, polylogue, what is written here is full to the brim of speaking voices. One of the great pleasures in putting together this anthology has been in discovering the interplay between voices, sometimes connecting, sometimes in counterpoint and contrast. And especially so between poetry and prose which, for many of the writers here, are not at all impermeable, the one flowing into the other, narrative and lyric voice meeting with fluent grace. The once 'loyal, polite and dutiful' daughters *(Rita Kelly)* are learning to show scant respect for any but the rythms and shape of their own lives and tongues. And do so with a deceptively casual directness which should never be mistaken for complacent ease.

'Ní maith liom cearca -
Bíonn boladh agus bús uathu -
Ach is maith liom an dá scéilín sin,
Agus is ar cearca a bhraitheann siad.'
(I don't like hens -
They are smelly and fussy -
But I like those two little stories,
And both are dependent on hens.)
                    (Máire Mhac an tSaoi)

The search for a language, a voice of our own, may be one of the reasons why Irish women are so strongly drawn towards poetry because, after all, 'poetry concerns taboos. Poetry is what we are not allowed to talk about' *(Medbh McGuckian)*. Because, it may be, poetry enables us to move outside and beyond that 'cobwebby state, chilled vault littered with our totems'(*Paula Meehan*) into which history and literary tradition have flung us.

It must surely be obvious but seems necessary to repeat, women and men are not identically positioned in relation to culture, history, politics. And although there will be significant points of intersection, common desires and dreams, the hunger for selfhood, wholeness, identity, call it what you will, must be negotiated and articulated differently in each case. What are women to do? Traditionally designated as powerless and voiceless, how are we to avoid distorting our realities, deforming our visions so that they merge with the mainstream and become indistinguishable from it? How also, or consequently, to escape what Medbh McGuckian has called 'the masochism of marginalisation'? How to speak without losing whatever slender vestige of ourselves has survived? 'I always feel very aware that I'm doing something that is traditionally a male preserve and that I'm trespassing, and that when I'm trespassing most successfully, it's because I'm turning into a man.......' (*Medbh McGuckian*). Creativity in whatever form is always in some measure subversive. How much more deeply and acutely so for a woman, who must break a double taboo, assert her presence both as woman and as artist.

The choices for Irish women have been traps. Write in terms and in a language the Other can accomodate and absorb — or hold your silence.

The writings in this collection break that age-old silence. They do not all confront, far less resolve, the facts and dilemmas of womanhood to the same extent. By no means all of them are self-consciously 'about' Irishness. On the contrary, they develop themes, use forms and structures, whether in fiction or in poetry, which disturb a tradition that would keep us, mere shadow dolls, 'under glass, under wraps' (*Eavan Boland*). And while each woman writes from a position where neither nationality nor gender can go entirely without saying, there is a refusal to write in terms of an idea of either. What it means to be a woman at this time, in this place, living, working, writing as diversely as we do, is not an idea but a reality, or more accurately, a whole series of realities. Realities not precluding imaginative transfiguration which may empower us, but rather providing foundations of truthfulness and passionate authenticity on which to build a future. For many of the writers here, realism is not a convention but an urgent need, not a constraint but a great and new freedom. Freedom to give a name and substance to the long unspoken, always unwritten, realities of their lives. For others, there is the equally pressing need to radically break with conventional forms of narrative, syntax or genre. In all, there is movement from what we have been to what we may become:

> 'The blackbird on this first sultry morning
> in summer, finding buds, worms, fruit,
> feels the heat. Suddenly she puts out her wing -
> the whole, full, flirtatious span of it.'
> *(Eavan Boland)*

Exploratory, innovative, assured in some, more tentative, elliptical, discrete in others.

Living and creating on the margin makes you sharp, tough, sometimes wise, but it's still a hard lonely, dangerous place to be. There is little room for compassion and none for the comfort of illusion. Purism, ideological or aesthetic, has no place in the world of those who struggle simply to survive. 'Some people know what it is like........And other people don't' *(Rita Ann Higgins)*. The prevalence of our own internalised barbarisms has to be acknowledged and confronted. They are not always easy to eradicate:

> 'I snarl over the carcass,
> not to warn them off
> but from my one
> terror....that this
> is no wild life
> but a Safari Park
> where a warden charts my progress.....'
> *(Roz Cowman)*

The margin leaves its scars on those who survive. And the survivors are often angry. 'There is an awful lot of rage and it's not just a personal rage, it's a transpersonal rage. It's my mother's rage and my mother's mother's rage and it goes back for generations.' (Nuala Ní Dhomhnaill) Of scars and anger we do not fear to speak, must speak, if we are to emerge from the frozen stillness of oppression:

> 'Mother. Step up from under that sod,
> push aside my father, that dirty earth

shove it off. I need to know what
you are doing there dead.'
(Ane Le Marquand Hartigan)

Women who write and who go on writing are by definition
survivors. Women who refuse, in and through their writing, to
accept the so-called truths imposed upon them are by definition
subversive. In this anthology Irish women themselves define the
terms of their survival and their subversion. Not according to
the word of the fathers. Probably not as our-mothers taught us
to do. Not, I suspect, always according to the expectations of our
sisters elsewhere. Assuredly not enough for our daughters. Can
it ever be enough?

Given the harshness, the plain injustice of our fate, there is
nothing to be wondered at in the force of our fury, in our need to
say it as it is, as we see it, as we live it. The miracle, surely, is that
there is yet enough energy and hope to imagine it as it could,
will, be. Still faith enough for a sense of continuity and
generosity to break through whatever inadvertent fissures can
be found. Still space for wit and humour and pleasure:

> 'The sky cracked
> And there was a huge laughter......'
> *(Eithne Strong)*

What I looked for in bringing together these writings was,
above all else, work which refused to be 'loyal, polite, dutiful',
work carrying the marks of our resistance thematically or
formally. I looked for writing which, without conforming to a
pre-determined agenda, was unashamedly rooted in the
experiences and politics of women's lives diversely lived. This is
not celebratory writing, certainly. There is too much suffering,
violence and anger still to be written over and through. Our
troubles are too raw to be denied and there is so much personal
history still to be recorded. 'I grew up with ghosts....' *(Clairr
O'Connor)*. At the same time, and most emphatically, Irish
women are not martyred Marys. These writers are in no sense
compliant or complaining victims. They are far too obstreporous
for that. Some are overtly iconoclastic or rebellious, others resist
through irony or bone-dry wit, a laconic edge to their voice. And
there is writing which is expressive of a kind of gentleness, not
sentimental, never genteel, all the more remarkable in a hard-
edged world.

14

There is here a profusion, even a willful confusion, of themes and perspectives, images and strategies; there are disagreements and affinities, certainties and insecurities. Pattern and meaning have always been imposed on women, from the outside. Only lately have we begun to openly protest the shaping of our self-hood. However much an anthologist is supposed to do so, it would be a betrayal for me to seek to impose patterns of sense and connection on work which is so various and still in process; a lie to smoothe over jagged, unresolved edges; dishonest to disguise the uncertainties which continue to undermine us. They must stand as they are, because that is, for the time being, the way it is.

But 'the future can always be rewritten' *(Linda Anderson).* Is being rewritten, by so many more women than I have been able to include here. The agony of selection, or,more precisely of omission, must surely be the greatest difficulty faced by anyone compiling an anthology. To include is by definition to exclude, and the criteria are not easy to set, even less to articulate. All of the writers here are Irish, in the most literal and ordinary sense of Ireland generally being the place where they were born and raised, live and work. But Ireland, need I say it, has a fraught history and a difficult present, so not all are Irish nationals, and a few now work abroad. Many of the contributors are well-known, and have published a good deal. Yet others are new (not necessarily 'younger'), relatively unpublished. All the contributors were entirely positive and enthusiastic about the project. Some who were invited to contribute could not accept because of other commitments, and their presence is missed. Only one or two declined, or failed to respond. I wanted, deliberately, to include poetry and fiction, partly because distinctions between genres reinforce hierarchies and prejudices we have as readers and critics, and partly because so many Irish women write in both genres anyway. I was sometimes surprised by what contributors sent to me - a story where I had expected poems, or the other way round. Most of the pieces were written specially for the anthology, although a few have appeared before, mainly in Ireland. There is work in Irish as well as in English, because we do, after all, have some capacity for choice.

This anthology virtually imposed itself, as a necessary statement of the fact of Irish women's writing now. A statement of its breadth and depth, its power and variety, in Irish and in English, in poetry and fiction. It is important for us to make that statement, because if we do not, our work will continue to be altogether denied, ignored or only grudgingly admitted to the jealously male-guarded territory of 'Irish literature'. I hope that this collection will help us to see that what Irish women are writing has substance and presence, courage and confidence, reclaiming something of our suppressed heritage, inventing possiblities for the future. And it is good for us and for others to know that we speak proudly, independently in an anthology published by an Irish women's press.

Irish women are gazing into the forbidden well, not out of bravado, but as a necessary strategy for our survival and well-being. 'Water returns, hard and bright, out of the faulted hills' *(Moya Cannon)*, to rise and rise, ever wilder, submerging old oppressions.

I hope that this anthology will be a channel through which strong passionate waters may flow and resource us all.

Ailbhe Smyth (August, 1989)

Rita Kelly

The Patriarch

My father was a butcher,
and before he killed his sheep
he beat them
about the head
with the sticking-knife,
held clenched in his fist.
I can still hear the wooden handle resound off the bone
and the sheep's eyes roll before me,
having smelt blood she tried to resist
being slaughtered -
of course it is a *she*: the meat is more tender.

With cattle he had a different tactic,
because a heifer could kill him
in that narrow cold slaughter-house,
so he took a very thick rope
(as I've seen holding tons of barge
to a mooring post along the canals of memory)
and laced it on her neck with frightened rage,
and drew the end through a huge link in the floor
and pulled that beast to her knees.
And then I should wrap that rope
about my childish waist
and keep all that vibrating flesh on its knees.
If I failed to keep my footing
he beat me across the face,
and through my silent tears
I saw him slow and distorted,
like a deliberate monster
load the humane killer —
a lovely name for a thick lump of deadly metal -
and place it on her forehead,
he squeezed the trigger and she fell
pulling the rope tighter about my waist,
but I could step towards her
and ease my pain, seeing the neat hole which never bled
above the dead open eyes.

17

The entrails of the dead beasts
warmed me in that place of terror
and their blood ran down my legs,
long before I woke to find
my own blood hot and sticky
between my legs.

Yes, my father was a butcher,
and kicked me down the stairs
before going to the slaughter-house
because he had no choice,
and I must know that I could not choose.
But he had all the strength,
and I kept my tiny rage
intact behind silent tears
until soon I overcame that too,
and there were no tears, just silence,
and blood dripping passed my eyes,
I saw him through it
and I saw red.

Was I four, or eight, or twelve,
when I loved him enough
to sit with him at the opera
and note his delicate skin
in the half-light, that handsome man,
that butcher for whom I felt so much:
even when they bound him
and took him away ungraciously
and called his dilemma by a clinical name,
I remained loyal, polite and dutiful
hiding my rage with life,
to visit and find his head wired
and his limbs kicking with electric shock.
This was treatment, I never saw it as revenge.

I felt only pity, deep unspeakable pity,
I glimpsed all the dead sheep and cattle
in him as he crawled along
the floor, on his hands and knees,
some rattling unvoiced awful sounds
in his throat, and his blue eyes rolled at me
as if life was being squeezed out of him:
    I stood in the middle of that cell

while he crawled about me
and I felt the blood run down my legs.

I did not know
that if you take an eye or a tooth,
even if for an eye or a tooth,
that you must suffer the trauma
of losing an eye or a tooth -
if you kill, if you butcher,
you must experience the trauma of
killing and butchering.

And still no choice.
Just wonderful intellectualisms
to convince myself
that I could cope
with being butchered:
that I could understand
and explain it, and bear no resentments
as his eyes challenged me
to free him from
the confines of his cell,
to love him that much
and play Verdi on my expensive hi-fi
just for him, and partake delightfully
in all that pleasure.
No bitterness.

I simply showed all my bitterness
and all my anger to others,
especially to those for whom
I protested love.
I protected him.

Then last week I found him
partly paralysed,
his thundering right fist hung limp.
No need now to burn out
any more brain cells,
that fist will never rise again
to strike the defenceless.

He is now defenceless,
as he grips a tripod stick
with his left hand

and tries to stand,
and move cautiously
across the floor.

I do not fear that fist,
nor that hard black shoe.
He can still strike me
with his tongue,
and his words cut much deeper
than his hard black shoe -
I find my footing,
feel all the strength
that he has lost
invade my right arm
down to the fingertips.
Then I take the wide forceful angle
and strike into his face,
I hear the resounding bone,
and his still handsome face
falls from me, his body sprawls
painfully against the floor -
and suddenly I am no longer
tethered by a thick rope
to a dead animal.

There is now more shock
in those blue eyes
than ever a raging beast
could cause breaking loose
in a slaughter-house.

I shall never look
into those eyes again on this earth,
and he knows before he dies
that I have chosen
finally not to be butchered.

Frances Molloy

Women Are The Scourge Of The Earth
(For Ruth Hooley)

There's some people will try to put the blame for what
happened on to me, but I'm not having that. I don't care what
that note said. I don't care what the neighbours say. If they think
I give a damn, then they're mistaken. That woman was
deranged all her life. She was taking tablets for years from the
doctor for her nerves. Feared she was to let the wains out to play
in case they got shot. Silly cow, I told her to catch herself on. If
anybodywanted to shoot the bloody wains, they could come
into the house and do it.

I don't care what any of them try to tell you, I never lifted a
finger to her in all the years I put up with her. Never mind what
that hussy next door tries to make out. The stories I could tell
you about her! You should see the odd assortment of characters
that comes and goes there when he's out at his work, the poor
bugger. There's no telling who or what fathered half that crowd
of cross-eyed brats of hers. I must say, it's always the likes of her
that does the talking. I can't imagine what kind of an eegit he is
to put up with her. She should be run out of the town. Many's a
better woman was tarred and feathered for far less. Shooting is
too good for the likes of her.

That note my Missus left, made out that I turned her mother
and sisters against her, but unbalanced and all as she was, she
was still fly enough not to mention why. Well, I'll tell you why,
so you'll not be labouring under any illusions about her. She was
carrying on with a fancy man. She thought I would never find
out when I was at my work, but a friend of mine spotted the
same car parked outside my house on the same day every week
and gave me the wink. I soon put a stop to it, I can tell you.

I'm not a mug like your man next door. I kicked his teeth right
down his throat and let her ladyship know that I would
debollocks the bastard on the spot if he ever came snooking
round my house again. I'll not be made a laughing stock of.

Her mother was flaming mad when I told her the way her
precious daughter was carrying on. She said she was no
daughter of hers and she'd never darken her door the longest
day she ever lived. To give the woman her dues, she was as
good as her word. She never set foot in my house from that day

21

till this. Every one of her sisters backed me at the time too.

The Missus was more deranged than ever after that, eating nothing but these fool tablets from the doctor. Walking through the house in a stupor half the day, never even bothering to change from her night clothes. She was pining for him. You didn't need to be very bright to see that. All the time she kept crying and lamenting about her mother and sisters and trying to get me to go and explain to them that her fancy man was only a friend. I told her I'd see her in hell first. It was her that had got herself into the fix and it was up to herself to get back out of it. I'm not going to be made a fool of.

Never mind your inquest to establish the cause of death. I'm here to defend my good name. The woman was deranged, that's the long, the tall and the short of it. I lived with her for fifteen years and I'm telling you now, she was never in her proper mind. I don't know what I was thinking about, having anything to do with the likes of her in the first place, when I think of some of the women I could have had my pick of. I could have done a lot better for myself and married a good strapping farmer's daughter with a bit of capital behind her. Indeed, I'll have you all know, I could have had any woman I wanted just for the asking.

And there's another thing I want to draw your attention to, just when I'm at it. A woman is supposed to obey her husband, is she not? She's supposed to do what he bids her, is she not? Isn't that what the law says? Isn't it wrote in the bible by the hand of the almighty himself? Well, that woman that you're holding your inquest into never done my bidding in her life. Never once in fifteen years did she do a single thing I told her. For example, I warned her to keep away from that woman next door. I didn't want no wife of mine consorting with her likes. But did she heed me? Like hell she did. My friend seen that trollop in having tea with her ladyship whenever I was out at my work. My blood still boils when I think about it. The likes of that trash sitting gossiping in my house and me out breaking my back to earn the money to entertain her. I soon put a stop to that too. I locked the doors to the house and took the keys with me to work every day for a month and let it be known to the madam next door that if she wanted to get into my house, she could try getting in through the window. That put a stop to her visits. I won't be made a fool of.

And there's something else you ought to know too. She turned them five wains of hers against me. Not one of them has a decent word to say to me now. That wee uppity lying bitch Una, went away and told the doctor yarns behind my back.

What do you think of that for respect then? Going away behind my back and in defiance of my orders, bringing doctors round the house to see the mother. That woman would be alive today if she'd seen far fewer doctors. It was all the fool tablets that she got from them that made her fall. That's where she got all her bruises from. I never laid a finger on her in my life.

Una is turned into a right snottery wee brat, and she will need to mind her step. She'll not always have the old granny's skirts to hide behind. Just let her wait till all this fuss dies down. A man has a legal right to his own wains. I'll let her know before I'm through, who her boss is. Who does she think puts the shoes on her feet? Who does she think puts the clothes on her back? Who does she think puts the food in her belly? Who does she think's been paying the rent all these years? The beloved fancy man, uncle Harry?

What do you think of that then, uncle Harry? Uncle Harry, if you don't mind. She brought her dear uncle Harry round to her old granny and poisoned her against me. Me and the mother-in-law had always got on well enough. Mine, I'm not saying she wasn't a terrible old battle-axe, for she was, but as the man says, I didn't have to live with her. Now that woman has known me for more than eighteen years, and still, she's prepared to take the word of a total stranger before mine. What do you think of that for loyalty then? I suppose she thinks she's mixing in high-brow society now because he works in an office and wears pansy clothes.

But you haven't heard the best of it yet, no, not by a long shot. Wait till you hear the story the brave fellow is putting about. He's trying to make out that he met me Missus at a meeting of some daft organisation that's for people who has been let out of the funny-farm. What's its name now? Let me think? It's called "Mental" or something. No, that's not right. And it wasn't called "Insane" either for it started with an M, I'm sure of that now. "Mine", that's what it's called. It's for people that's out of their mines. "Mine", that's what its name is. Didn't I say it began with an M? You see, I was right.

He told the mother-in-law that me Missus was suffering from depression and that's why she joined this daft organisation of freaks. He tries to make out that he was suffering from depression too, and that's how the pair of them met. According to him, they were only friends, and it helped them if they came together for a chat and a cup of tea every week. What do you think of that for invention? Isn't it wile touching wouldn't you say? They were only friends indeed. I'd say he must have been very hard up for a friend if he had to rely on her.

The old granny is doting now, for didn't she swally the whole story, lock, stock and bloody barrel. You should hear her lamenting about how she should never have doubted for a minute, the virtue of her lily-white daughter. All he called for was a chat and a cup of tea! What does he take me for, a real dodo? That's the kind of story nobody but an old doting woman would fall for.

Depressed, indeed, a quare lot she had to be depressed about, I can tell you, with a mug like me out humping bricks on his back all day long to keep her in style. Carpets in every room that woman had. When I think about it yet, my blood still boils. Me out slaving from early morning till late at night to provide grandeur for her to impress her fancy man with.

I'll tell you this now, she's the last woman I'll ever fork out for. Women, they're all the same, after what they can get out of you. There's only one thing a woman is useful for and that's on the broad of her back. Nobody but a fool would marry a woman for that nowadays. There's plenty of it going free and no mistaking. I'm well rid of her. Women are the scourge of the earth. I've learnt my lesson. Once bitten, twice shy, as the man says.

Moya Cannon

Holy Well

Water returns, hard and bright,
out of the faulted hills.

Rain that flowed
down through the limestone's pores
until dark streams hit bedrock,
now finds a way back,
past the roots of the ash,
to a hillside pen
of stones and statues.

Images of old fertilities
testify to nothing more, perhaps,
than the necessary miracle
of water trapped and stored
in a valley where water is fugitive.

A chipped and tilted Mary
grows green among rags and sticks.
Her trade dwindles —
bad backs, rheumatic pains,
the supplications, mostly, and the confidences of old age.
    But sometimes
    swimming out in waters
    that were blessed in the hill's labyrinthine heart
    the eel flashes past.

Foundations

Digging foundations for a kitchen,
a foot and a half below the old concrete
they open a midden of seashells.

This used to be called "kitchen" —
poor man's meat, salty, secretive,
gathered at neap tide.

Blue mussels creaked as a hand twisted them from the cluster,
limpets were banged off with a stone, lifted with a blade,
the clam's breathing deep in wet sand
gave a mark to the spade.

And now this second exhumation,
in my backyard.
Six barrowloads are shovelled out and dumped,
the steel is positioned, the concrete ready to pour.

Packed shells run under into the neighbour's ground,
the party wall rests still
on a foundation of limpet-shells, mussels, clams.

Eros

To be with you, my love,
is not at all like being in heaven
but like being in the earth.

    Like hazelnuts we sleep
    and dream faint memories of a life
    when we were high, green among leaves —
    a life given
    in a time of callow innocence,
    before storms came
    and we all fell down,
    rattled down cold streams,
    caught in the stones,
    while berries, seasons flowed past.
    Then quicker currents, elvers, dislodged us,
    nudged us out into the flow,
    rushed us down with black leaf-debris,
    and swept on
    forgetting us
    on some river-bed or delta.

For us, drifted together,
this is the time when shells are ready
for that gentler breaking.

    The deep and tender earth
    assails us with dreams,
    breaks us,
    nourishes us,
    as we tug apart
    its own dark crust.

Mary Beckett

Heaven

To Hilary in her sixties, heaven was an empty house. She loved to come in from shopping and shut the door behind her knowing that there was nobody in any of the seven neat rooms and that nobody would arrive home until her husband did, shortly after six. A daughter-in-law might wish to call on her for some service but she had insisted from the beginning that they telephone first to arrange a suitable time. She noticed sometimes her opposite neighbour being visited by people who turned the key in the door and walked in. That, to Hilary, would have been intolerable. Occasionally someone said to her that she must be lonely with her four sons grown and gone. She smiled and murmured something about keeping busy and anyway when her sons were healthy and happy that was all that mattered.

She had appeared always as a devoted mother. When she was young her pram had been polished, the pillow immaculate, the blankets fluffy, the baby perfect. The nappies on the line were white and square like a television advertisement. The standard in the district was high except for a few unfortunate backsliders but Hilary was out on her own. Her little boys playing with the other children got dirty in the normal way but it was obviously newly acquired dirt on clean clothes, not general grubbiness. She was fortunate perhaps in that they all had her blonde pink-and-white appearance. None of them had inherited their father's dark hair and shadowed skin although they were tall like him and thin. Hilary often said then that she should slim but instead she dressed in drifty floaty clothes, and before hats went out of fashion she wore black gauzy hats with red cherries, or pink hats with veils or green hats with roses. She dressed up every afternoon to wheel out the pram and do the shopping. Some of the neighbours admired her style and others criticised that, but admitted she had great spirit.

The effort of all this perfectionism drained her each day so that when the children were eventually in bed she sat down by the fire and her husband sat in the opposite chair and she glanced at magazines and ate sweets and sighed or yawned every now and again. He read the papers in their entirety and switched the television from snowy channel to foggy channel

29

and back so that it blared all evening until they closed down for the night. At least then the noise came from one place only. Later, when the boys were in their teens, Hilary had to tolerate transistors in the bedrooms and tape-recorders as well as the television and record-player. So long as she stayed in her kitchen she had some slight refuge but it was there that the younger boys brought their troubles with sums, or spellings to hear or Irish passages to learn, while the older ones brought their complaints about unfair teachers or biased referees.

These worried her. It upset her to see their soft curved mouths drawn down in ugly resentment. She tried to persuade them not to feel aggrieved so readily, that it would become a habit and give them indigestion. She had to laugh them out of it because they would have been very embarrassed if she had confessed that she feared the harm it would do their souls. She never said such things to anyone. The only time she spoke out was at a parents' meeting once in the boys' school. There had been an alarming increase in rugby injuries to boys' spines, not in the school but in the country generally, news of brilliant boys paralysed for life. Some of the parents asked the priests who ran the school how their boys were safeguarded. The priests marshalled reassurances and the parents failed to put forward sensible objections. Hilary said she thought rugby an uncivilised game anyway and the rivalry between schools concerning rugby and between the priests involved was completely unchristian. There was a murmur of dissent and then several men shouted no, no.

"If anything happens to any of my boys on the rugby field" Hilary persisted, "I will go and howl outside the priests' house day and night." The other parents laughed but Hilary did not laugh and the priests did not really laugh either and none of her boys made much progress at rugby from that time on.

They did well at everything else, much better in their exams than their teachers ever expected going by their class marks and by their judgments to Hilary during parent-teacher meetings. They went to university and years followed of counting every penny to keep them there, of going without new clothes, of wearing cheap shoes long after they were broken and spread. Her husband had to keep his old car when it was a daily torment of refusing to start in the mornings or even at traffic lights, and people pushing it and looking as if they might get heart attacks. But they did well, so that their father often wondered aloud how far he too might have gone in this world if he had got the chances they were getting. Hilary never had such thoughts about herself. She fed them nourishing food morning and night, worried about their not having enough sleep, listened to their panics about exams, and to relieve the terrible feelings of impotence she had about them began going to Mass every morning to pray for their success. Then they were all finished with jobs except the youngest who was awarded a grant to do a PhD in an American university and insisted on marrying before he went, to his father's disgust. He fumed and fussed and denounced it as lunatic but Hilary was relieved because she had read novels about American universities and she could hardly believe such depravity existed. A wife would keep him safe.

Even before the others married she found herself alone in the house for long hours during the day. At first she would stand in the hall with her hands clasped, looking into empty rooms and wondering how she would celebrate. She generally finished up making herself tea and cake or eating a bar of chocolate with a feeling that there was something she was missing. Gradually she realised that this was not an occasional luxury, this solitude, but a routine. So she fixed a time every morning to sit and relish the quiet. As the days passed she grew more intense about it so that frequently the blood surged in her ears and she was whirled into a great cone of silence and stayed there suspended. She had no thoughts, no contemplations. She was not aware of the happiness it induced until she resumed her household activities and found herself smiling. She began hurrying home in the mornings to shut herself in. Only years of discipline insisted that she cleaned, washed and cooked as she always did. Sometimes the silence caught her up out of doors so that she drifted past people without seeing them or speaking to them.

She began thinking of heaven. She imagined deep silence. Innumerable people stood in rapture, no one touching another, backed and divided by pillars and arches as in Renaissance paintings, drawn, she supposed, to God whom she could not imagine, but still and complete in themselves. She was confident she was going there, seeing herself as a middle-aged to elderly ewe in the middle of the flock, giving no trouble at all to the shepherd. She had never had any great temptations; she was unlikely, she thought, to have any now. At funeral masses she happily saw herself as the dead person and arranged in her mind how things should be done about food, flowers and cars. No one would miss her, she had done all that had been asked of her, she could fade out any time.

She did do baby-sitting for the grandchildren any time she was asked until her eldest son took his wife off for a holiday to celebrate her getting a job, and left their three year old boy with Hilary for a fortnight. Before the first week was over she was consumed by the same desire for perfection in everything to do with this grandson as with her sons more than twenty years before. His hair must shine, his teeth must gleam, his clothes must grace his little straight sturdy body. When she watched him concentrating on a toy she contemplated the possibility of his being lonely at any time in the future or unhappy or unsuccessful and could hardly bear the pain. When her son came to collect him after his holiday he congratulated her on the child's fine appearance.

"It'll be all right to leave him round on Monday morning when Pauline and I are going to work, won't it?" he asked casually and Hilary said, "No, not at all," sharply, and then made excuses that she was too old, that he'd be better in his own home with someone to look after him.

"We don't know anybody suitable," her son protested, "It's risky to let in someone we don't know, she might not care for him properly."

"He is your child" she said tartly. "He is your responsibility, yours and Pauline's. You cannot shift it on to me. You'll just have to pay somebody well and hope for the best."

He seized on that, "But we had every intention of paying you. Of course we had. You mustn't think ..." "How much would you have thought of? Five pounds a week? No no no, money wouldn't make any difference." They had actually thought that if there were any question of money they should offer twenty pounds a month — it would be better paid by the month, but that indeed it was unlikely she would take any money. What would she want money for? She never bought anything except just the necessary food. She would be so glad of the child's company during her long empty day. He would give her a fresh interest in life and they'd collect him most evenings after work.

They did not forgive her. The child was left in a playschool in the mornings and collected by a neighbour who minded him with her own children until his parents came home. It was not satisfactory, really. Hilary, after a week or two of sleepless nights managed to put him out of her mind most of the time. A year later, tidying a drawer she came across a silly affectionate birthday card given to her by one of her sons when they were young and she felt a pang. It was nice after all when she was of use to them so that they loved her.

One morning her husband opened a letter that made him laugh first and then angered him. "What is it?" she asked with only a polite interest. He hesitated for a minute and then handed it over. It said,

"Dear Sir, You should know your wife is an alcoholic. She is being talked about all over the district. She hurries home in the mornings without talking to her neighbours and shuts herself in the house. Some of these days she will disgrace you.
Signed.

A Wellwisher."

She was alarmed even though they had mistaken the object of her addiction.

"I shouldn't have shown it to you" he said, looking at her in surprise. "It's upset you. Sure we all know you drink nothing but coffee and tea although you drink plenty of them. It's only some crank." He was watching her though, and when he came home from work he continued to watch her. He suggested they go for a walk. She refused, murmuring something about tired feet. The next night he thought they should go for a drive. She hadn't been in the car for years except for Sunday mass or Friday night shopping.

"What would we do that for?" she asked, embarrassed. "It's threatening rain."

The attention unnerved her making it more difficult for her to escape into her silence but she could cope so long as he was there only in the evening. Then he retired. She had known for years the date of his retirement but refused to face it, as did he.

He would give full attention to the garden, he said, and he tramped in and out of her kitchen, needing water when she was at the sink, wanting her hand to hold a line for beds he was digging. He grunted and groaned and held his hand to the small of his long back. He didn't enjoy it. He had no company. His dark face grew more and more saturnine. Hilary dreaded coming home to him. He had stopped watching her but he continued the recent invitations to walks, drives, meals out. They were no longer a lifeline for her but for himself. She refused, regardless. She had always an excuse: she was tired, she had no clothes. She had never revived her interest in clothes, suppressed while the money was needed for her growing family. She wore black trousers with an elastic waistband and any kind of tunic on top. He urged her to buy something else but she put it off.

One rainy day when he was sitting in the kitchen, rubbing continuously at the threadbare places on the knees of his trousers he asked "Hilary, why did you marry me?"

"Such a thing to ask, out of the blue" she said, taken aback. "Have you nothing better to think about than ancient history?"

"It's not ancient history. Whatever there was then surely keeps on now. You don't love me now: you can't stand me around the place. Did you love me ever, that's what I want to know. That's what I have to know."

"For goodness' sake it's just that I'm not used to somebody under my feet in the daytime. You're miserable yourself - you should think of something to get you out among other men."

"You're not answering me," he kept on so that she snapped at him "And I'm not going to answer you. How can I remember what it was like when I was young?"

He said no more but sat there, hunched.

She was uncomfortable, remembering clearly what it was like to see her twenties speeding by and in spite of her blonde hair and pink cheeks and Ballybunion and Salthill and Tramore and numerous escorts nobody had offered to marry her. She had seized on the prospect of marriage with him as the only way to a real life - her old life had no sense or meaning. They had been well suited, neither until now interested in the other. She had her children, her house and then her silence. He had his job and his children to a certain extent. Now he had nothing and, she thought indignantly, he was busy seeing that she'd have nothing either.

While he was about the house she never sat down until night-time, she polished and cleaned things that were already shining. She hovered over the cooker as it cooked their simple meals. He was either in the kitchen reading his paper or in and out of the garden. His breathing banished silence from the house. The smallest sounds impinged on her, the gentle bong of the Venetian blind upstairs at an open window, the click of a thermostat in the bathroom as it turned itself on or off, the ticking of clocks all over the house, unsynchronised.

Before the winter set in she told the priest at her monthly confessions, "I have feelings of hatred for my husband, murderous feelings. I am afraid I will do him an injury — I have carving knives and heavy casseroles in the kitchen." The priest told her to pray about it, to see a doctor, to get a hobby for herself or her husband. "But" he warned her "Don't let hatred enter into your soul or you'll be fighting it until your dying day." She was afraid then of losing her peace in heaven as well as the peace in her home. All the beautiful broad shining avenues of silence would be shut off from her and she would be condemned to some shrieking cacophonous pit.

She urged the buying of a garden shed and a greenhouse to occupy him. He was not enthusiastic about them but he consented after long deliberations on the back mat over where

34

they were to go and then what was to go in them. She tried putting a chair in the shed and bringing out his morning coffee and afternoon tea, but she could not put him out of her mind. Every time she glanced out of the window she could see his shape, stooped. She could even see the sun sparkling on the drip at the end of his nose.

She resigned herself and rang up her daughters-in-law. "I will mind your children after play-school" she told them. "I need my mornings for messages and housework but I'll have them on a regular basis from lunch-time until you come home from work. I don't want any money for it. Their grandfather can collect them. He'll help me with them. I'll not find them too much for me while he is there." They were stiff. They were dubious.

"You would need to be sure you're not just using our children to cover your own loneliness" Pauline said.

"I have never been lonely Pauline, never in my life" she answered mildly, so they allowed themselves to be persuaded and every afternoon five children aged between two and six invaded her life.

She had one of her sons go up to the roof-space and bring down all the toys and books that were stored there since his own childhood and because there were no girls' playthings she produced her old green and rose petalled hats so that they could dress up. She put a load of builders' sand in the back garden and saw it tramped everywhere. She was vigilant that they didn't rub it into one another's eyes or use the spades as weapons. She hugged them when they cried and loved their hot damp foreheads pressing into her neck. After their tea she sorted them out from the debris, packed them into the car and her husband delivered them to their three separate homes. Apart from collecting and delivering the children he took no interest in them. When the elder son of his eldest son put his hand on his knee and said, "Come on out and kick football, Grandfather" he almost blushed but made an excuse and went up to the bathroom, no refuge with five children in the house. One evening he told her that he was tired of the arrangement, too old to suffer all those children. He would still act as chauffeur but he had met another grandfather at the playschool and they had decided to go to a bowling-green not far away on good evenings and to a quiet pub if it rained. He would not be at home in the afternoons for the foreseeable future. There were plenty of things to do for a retired man still active and alert. Hilary agreed, told him he was perfectly right, and sat down exhausted every evening when she had cleaned up the mess left by the children, far too tired to do anything but leaf through a magazine or glance now and then at her husband's choice of television programmes, six clear channels now, one always blaring.

Now and again, though, she did catch a distant glimpse of calm corridors and vaulted roofs all soundless and it gave her a feeling of great sweetness in anticipation.

Leland Bardwell

Them's Your Mother's Pills

They'd scraped the top soil of the gardens
and every step or two they'd hurled a concrete block
Bolsters of mud like hippos from the hills
rolled on the planters plantings of the riff-raff of the city.

The schizophrenic planners had finished off their job
folded their papers, put away their pens —
The city clearances were well ahead.

And all day long a single child was crying
while his father shouted: Don't touch them,

Them's your mammie's pills.

I set to work with zeal to play "Doll's House",
"Doll's Life", "Doll's Garden", while my adolescent sons played
"Temporary Heat"
in the sitting room out front
and drowned the opera of admonitions:

Don't touch them, them's your mammie's pills.

Fragile as needles the women wander forth
laddered with kids, the unborn one ahead
to forge the mile through mud and rut
where mulish earth-removers rest, a crazy sculpture.

They are going back to the city for the day
this is all they live for —
Going back to the city for the day.

The line of shops and solitary pub
are camouflaged like check points on the border
the supermarket stretches emptily
a circus of sausages and time
the till-girl gossips in the veg department
Once in a while a woman might come in
to put another pound on
the electronic toy for Christmas.

From behind the curtains every night
the video lights are flickering, butcher blue
Don't touch them, them's your mammie's pills

No one has a job in Kilenarden
nowadays they say it is a no-go area
I wonder, then, who goes and does not go
in this strange forgotten world
of video and valium

I visited my one time neighbour
not so long ago. She was sitting
in the hangover position
I knew she didn't want to see me
although she'd cried when we were leaving

I went my way
through the quietly rusting motor cars and prams
past the barricades of wire, the harmony of junk.
The babies that I knew are punk-size now
and soon children will have children
and new voices ring the *leit motif*:

Don't touch them, them's your mammie's pills.

Exiles
(To Geraldine O'Reilly)

Those were the seedlings we sowed
pricked and primed
against the rock of poverty.
We have put names on their children
The children
of Gurley Flynn and Mother Jones
Oh your america.

Tumbletown and dead river valley
famine-forced they crowded the canals
from the Bog of Allen to Idaho,
crossed the Atlantic
in the stench of homelessness.

Now Bridie don't forget to say your prayers

Mother get me a bride
from out the four green fields
(my fields).

Mean fields.

Some got the lace
others fell like stones
uselessly

And ... to hell with the broken fingers
cooking fat at night
by candle quiver
We'll show you who the boss is
(a nickel a day, make hay make hay)
you Irish bitches ...

Now Bridie keep your legs crossed
and the rosary between your toes

Give me your fat.

But they rose ... rose ...
like bonfires on a mountain
every mansheila of them
rose against the whips
broke files, made unions.
It was a slow going
a slow coming.

Dear Bridie I received the dollars
your father's taken ill
I got shoes for Peadar
and Kathleen
I'll put the rest by
Pray for me

Why are we waiting
get me the DC.9
New York, New World
New suitcase, transit visa

Dear Uncle Tom get me a husband
and a Green card
And I'll never never leave
your america

My Green Card —

Mean Card.

This is your pilot
Pointing Pilot
Feathering down on Kennedy Airport

Oh america

I strike out now
in a skyscrape of desire
shivering for dollars

You mean I've come all the way from Clontarf
And there's no job?

Suffered under pointing pilot
Why does everyone sleep
in the subway?

Maeve Kelly

Orange Horses

Elsie Martin's husband beat her unconscious because she called him twice for his dinner while he was talking to his brother. To be fair, she did not simply call him. She blew the horn of the Hiachi van to summon him.

He had never beaten her unconscious before. He was surprised and a little frightened when she lay down and did not get up. He was a small man but she was even smaller, weighing barely seven stone, and she was further handicapped by being five months pregnant. Afterwards, his mother said that if Elsie had fed herself better, instead of wasting good money on them fags she'd have been able to take the few wallops and got over them the way any normal woman would.

"He didn't mean nothin'," the elder Mrs Martin said. "He got a bit ahead of himself. But she shouldn't have blown the horn at him that way. A man won't take that kind of treatment from any woman and I wouldn't expect him to. He has his pride."

She leaned on the caravan door while she spoke, staring out at the twisted remains of a bicycle, a rusty milk churn, a variety of plastic containers, three goats, two piebald ponies, all tethered to an iron stake, and a scattering of clothes hanging on the fence which separated her domain from the town dump. Behind her, Elsie lay stretched. Her jaw had been wired in the hospital and was still aching. The bruises on her legs were fading and the cut in her head had been stitched and was healing nicely now, thank God.

"You'll be grand again, with the help of God," her mother-in-law said, watching the ponies reach for a fresh bit of grass on the long acre. "Grand," she repeated with satisfaction, as if by saying the word she made it happen, God's help being instantly available to her. "You're grand. I'll be off now and I'll cook him a bit myself. I'll get one of the young ones to bring you over a sangwich. You could manage a sangwich."

Elsie closed her eyes trying to squeeze out the pain. Her stomach had not shrunk back to normal. The baby was only gone a week. She folded her hands over the place where he had been. She was sure he had been a boy, the way he kicked. She grieved quietly for him, for his little wasted life that never got the chance to be more than a few small kicks and turns inside her body. But she was sorry for herself too, because she had a feeling about him, that he would be good to her. He might have been the one to protect her when the others were married with their own wives. She could tell by the older boys that they would hit their wives to control them. She wouldn't interfere but she would not stay around to watch her history being repeated. She had planned a life for herself with this baby. The plan would have to be changed.

Brigid, her eldest daughter, stepped lightly into the caravan and stood beside her. "Nana says would you like a drink of tay with your sangwich."

"Shut the door," Elsie said crossly. "You're letting the wind in. And sweep out the place. Didn't I tell you to do it this morning? Do you ever do anything you're told?"

"I did it. Them childer have it destroyed on me."

"Who's minding them? Are they all at your Nana's? Where's Mary Ellen? Where's your father?"

"I dunno." The child took the sweeping brush and began to sweep the floor. Her sullen expression annoyed her mother almost more than the careless way she swept the bits of food through the caravan door and out onto the green. A dog poked hopefully through the crumbs, then looked up expectantly at Brigid. She said "geraway outa that," without enough conviction for him to move. He placed a paw on the step. She pushed it off and stared maliciously at him. "I'll tell my Daddy on you, you little hoor," she whispered and then, a living image of her grandmother, leaned on the brush handle surveying the scene.

"Look, Mama," she called. "The sky is orange. Why is it orange?"

Elsie lay back, floating between waves of pain, bathing herself in its persistence. She tried anticipating its peaks, the way she had been learning to anticipate the peaks in labour pains for the baby who was born dead. For the first time in her sixteen years of child bearing she had attended an ante-natal class. It had all come to nothing. She should have known better. Her husband hadn't wanted her to go. He had been persuaded by the social worker to let her try it. But he had grumbled a lot after her visits and told her she was getting too smart. "Baby or no baby," he said, "you're due a beating. Keeping in with the country people isn't going to do you any good. And they don't care for you anyway. You're only a tinker to them."

She turned her head to see what Brigid was up to. The child had dropped the brush and was standing very still staring at something.

"What are you staring at?" the mother called.

"The pony is orange too," Brigid said softly. "The pony is orange."

She had cross eyes of a strange pale grey and the glow of the sunset lit them and changed their colour to a near yellow. One of the ponies suddenly tossed his head and flicked a quick look in her direction before turning his attention back to his patient grazing. Brigid wondered what it would be like to ride him. She was never allowed to try. If she did, her brothers knocked her off. She was beginning to think that she didn't want to ride. She would soon forget that she had ever had such a desire. Her brothers rode like feudal lords, galloping through wastelands and even through the crowded streets, proud and defiant. Brigid fixed her sombre gaze on the pony's back. It must be like the wind, she thought. It would be like racing the wind. That's why her brothers were so proud and cocky. They could race the wind, and she couldn't. Her father did it once. Her mother never did it. Her mother got beaten and had babies and complained. Her mother was useless.

Elsie called out,"What are you sulking about now? Would you take that look off your face? If you can't do anything for me would you go away and leave me in peace."

When she was gone, Elsie wanted her back. "Brigid," she cried hopelessly, "Brigid." It was a pity she wasn't loveable so that Elsie could cuddle her and tell her she was sorry for being cross. But what was the point? Brigid was eleven years of age and she should be doing things for her mother. What did she do all day? Gave them their breakfast in the morning and pushed the small ones in the buggy, but beyond that — nothing. She spent most of the day moping around, listening to the gossip in the other caravans.

The caravans were arranged in a circle around the small caravan owned by Hannah, Elsie's mother-in-law. When her children married and had their own caravans they took their place in the circle whenever they came for a gathering. Their father was dead. There were nine surviving sons and seven daughters. When the father was sixty he stopped beating Hannah and got religion very bad. He paid frequent visits to the holy nun in the convent who could cure everything but death. He died peacefully, like a baby asleep and had a huge funeral. From England and Scotland and all over Ireland the relations came to bury him. The casualty department in the hospital was kept going for two days with the results of their mourning. Hannah was very proud though she wept for weeks, being supported by all her daughters and all but two of her daughters-in-law, Elsie and Margaret Anne.

Elsie remembered Margaret Anne, the way she used to drink the bottles of tawny wine so that she wouldn't feel the beatings. One night she drank a full bottle of vodka and choked in her own vomit. She was twenty three. There were no fights after her funeral. There was no lamentation. Her children cried and her husband cried and took the pledge for six months. Two years later he married her youngest sister and they went away to England. There were plenty of sites in London for them. They would simply break down a gate, pull the caravan in and stay put until they were evicted. England, Elsie's youngest sister said, was a grand place. They had been put up in the best hotels for months because they were homeless.

Elsie often thought of staying in the best hotels too. Her husband called it one of her notions. His sisters said "that one has too many notions." She had notions about not wanting to do the houses with them, about not wanting to stay home, night after night, while her husband went drinking with his brothers. The worst notion of all was when she arranged to get her dole money split so that she got her own share and the share for half the children. The Welfare Officer gave her dire warnings that if she changed her mind again, as she had done before, she would be left with nothing. Her husband coaxed, threatened and beat her but she would not surrender. She had notions about Fonsie when she met him at the horse fair in Spancel Hill. Her parents had pulled their caravan into a by-road a few miles from the village. It was a scorching day when she saw Fonsie tussling with a colt, backing him up, jerking his head to show his teeth, running his hands down his fetlocks, slapping his flanks. The animal reared and bucked and frightened bystanders.

"Aisy, aisy," a farmer said. "You'll never sell him that way,"
"I'm not asking you to buy him," Fonsie said smartly.

"You're not, for I wouldn't," said the man. "I never saw any good come from a tinker."

"You wouldn't have the price of him," Fonsie said and turned his head and winked at Elsie. His red hair was like a mad halo and his eyes were a blazing blue. She was like a rabbit hypnotised by a weasel. She followed him everywhere. She badgered her parents until they consented to the wedding. She was fifteen. She ignored all their warnings about his bad blood. He was the middle of the brothers and above and below him they were all the same. Always drinking. Always in trouble. Always dodging the law, frequently in jail or facing the judge and getting some smart solicitor to get them off on a technicality.

Fonsie never went to jail. He was too smart. But he didn't

want her to be too smart. "Smart women annoy me," he said. "So be smart and stay stupid." One night when she was three months pregnant, he hit her because she was too smart by half, an ugly bitch who gave him the eye at Spancel Hill and was probably after being with someone else and the child could be anyone's.

There were different notions in her head then when she picked herself up from the floor and cried for her own people who were travelling up north. Through one of her sisters-in-law she got word to her own sisters. One of them travelled to see her and give her advice.

"Don't be saying anything to him when he is drunk."

"I didn't say anything," Elsie said.

"Well maybe you should have. Did you look at him? A man can hate a hard look. He'll take it as an insult.".

"I looked at the floor," Elsie said. "I was afraid to look at him."

"Well there you are then. That's how it happened," her sister said triumphantly. "You didn't spake to him and you didn't look at him. Sure that explains it."

"He says the child isn't his."

"An old whim he has. His brothers putting him up to it. They're too much together. They should be at home with their wives instead of always in each other's company. They're terrible stuck on each other."

Elsie knew that was the trouble. A man was alright on his own with a woman but put him in with the herd of men, especially the herd of his own family and he lost his senses.

Her sisters had always given her plenty of advice. "Don't get too fat or you won't be able to run away when he wants to bate you. Learn the houses that are good to travellers. Don't try them too often. Don't look for too much the first time. Always bring a baby with you. If you haven't one, borrow one. Keep half of the money for yourself." Her mother gave her one piece of advice. "Keep silent and never show a man the contempt you feel for him. It is like spitting in the face of God."

It was good advice, especially the bit about the money. Her sisters had not told her how to keep the money, where to hide it, what to do with it. For them that was the simplest part. They could thrust their hands down into the recess between their breasts and pull up a wad of notes worth a couple of hundred pounds. When a caravan was needed their men would call on them as others would call on a Banker. Their interest rates were negotiable and were never paid in kind but in behaviour or favours granted. Her sisters knew how to control their husbands, but they were simple men and not as cute as hers. He always seemed to know when she had money accumulated and usually managed to beat it out of her. His spies were everywhere, his sisters and mother always prying and asking questions of the children. She stopped bringing the small children on her rounds. In spite of warnings, it was easy for them to let out important information, like where she had been for the few hours of her absence. Elsie knew that she was one of the best of the travellers for getting money from the settled people. They liked her because she was polite and handsome and clean. She didn't whine and she didn't exaggerate. Pride and a certain loyalty to her own people wouldn't allow her to tell the truth about her husband's drinking and beatings. For some of her regulars it wasn't necessary. Her black eyes and bruises were enough.

The latest accumulation was lying under a stone in the mud bank, twenty paces from her caravan. £353 in twenty pound notes and ten pound notes and five pound notes and one pound notes. She had counted it lovingly, feeling the notes, smoothing them out, folding them into twenty pound bundles held in place by elastic bands, the whole lot wrapped in a plastic supermarket bag. If her husband moved the caravan her treasure was still measurable. It was thirty five paces from the third cement pole, holding the last section of fencing around the dump. If someone moved the poles, it was a hundred paces from the bend in the new road. If the country people decided to change the road, as she knew from experience was a likely occurrence, it was two hundred paces from the last brick house on the estate. If that went, then it was straight under the last rays of the setting sun on 23 September. If there was no sun on 23 September she would dig the bank from dump to road in the middle of the night until she found it. If there was no bank ... If someone came with a bulldozer ... She sat up suddenly. She wanted to rush out to claw at the clay, scrabbling like a dog crazy for his buried bone, in the mud and bare rooted trees.

She lay down again, her secret like a flame to be kept alive but not so alive that it would leap up and consume her. At long last she had learned discipline. At long last she had learned her mother's secret of silence. When she used the Hiachi horn she almost broke the secret. The sound of the horn had its own words and her husband understood them. Only that morning he had looked at her and said "You're due a beating and when I have time I'll give it to you." She should have been there waiting for him, dinner ready, whenever he turned up. She should always wait around the caravan, never further away from his mother's or his sisters' vans. He didn't like her going to his brothers' vans where she might gossip or plot treason with their wives, or worse, be unfaithful with one of the brothers.

Once only had Elsie and the sisters-in-law plotted. The great idea came to them that they would run away together and leave all the children to Hannah. There were forty three children under the age of twelve. They sat contemplating the idea in wonder on a sunny morning when the men had gone to collect their dole money and the sisters were gossiping with Hannah. The idea had been thrown out by Mary Teresa and when the magic of it had been chewed over and gloried in it was Mary Teresa who began to destroy it. She said, "My Danny would never be able to look after himself." After that it was a landslide of surrender. Kathleen said her two boys were wild already and if she left them to their father, no knowing what would become of them. They'd end up in trouble with the law. Bridie said her fellow wouldn't take a bite from anyone only herself. Eileen said "Mine are all at school. He'd never bother sending them and they'd lose all the schooling they had." And she'd never mind them, meaning Hannah. "She's all talk. When it comes down to it she won't look after another woman's children even if they are her grandchildren. All talk, that's all she is." Elsie thought uncomfortably of Brigid and how she hadn't got around to giving her all the loving she should have done and how her father had eyed her a few times but she couldn't put that thought into words. She said, "I'd be worried about Brigid." Then suddenly all the women remembered their daughters in surprise and confusion and began to name them off, one by one, picturing each child, pretty or plain, cross-eyed or red haired, loving or deviant, as if naming them became their remembrance.

Elsie lay thinking about all of this as the sunset deepened into a scarlet glow, filling the caravan with its radiance, bouncing off her brass ornaments and mirrors, turning her faded blanket into a brilliant rug, a kaleidoscope of purest wonder. She dozed for a while, soothed by the sun's strange lullaby. She was disturbed by shouts and the thunder of hooves around the caravan. She twitched the curtain to peer out. The magic had gone out of the sky but over the town the pale shape of a crescent moon could just be seen. The pickers were beginning to set fire to the dump and its acrid-smelling smoke drifted in a long low swathe towards the housing estate. The cries of children at a last game before bedtime reached her and above them came the shouts of her two eldest sons who waved their arms and ran after one of the piebald ponies. As Elsie peered through the window, she could see the animal tearing away into the distance, towards the high church steeple, with its rider hanging on for dear life.

More trouble, Elsie thought. Someone had stolen the pony. Then the door was pushed in and Johnny and Danny burst upon her, pulling at her blankets, crying, "get up, get up, Brigid has taken the pony." Fonsie was after them, face red with rage shouting, "that's your rearing for you, the little bitch has gone off riding like a tinker on the piebald."

Well then, thought Elsie, stroking her wired up jaw, here's a right how do ye do. The little bitch is up on a pony and away like the wind.

"Wait till I lay hands on the little rap," Fonsie said bitterly. "Bringing disgrace unto the whole family. She's your daughter alright. But is she mine? Answer me that will you?"

"She is yours," Elsie said. "She didn't get that wild blood from me. Did you ever see one of my sisters up on a pony? Have any of my family got red hair? Every one of us has brown eyes. 'Twasn't from the wind she got the blue eyes and the hair."

"She could be Danny's. From day one he was hanging around you. From the minute I brought you back."

"He was twelve then," Elsie said wearily, playing the chorus to an old tune.

"What has that got to do with it? You were fifteen. Brigid's near twelve now. She's not like a girl at all. There could be something wrong with her. When your jaw is better let you see to it and when she gets back here, I'll give her a lesson she won't forget. Don't give me any of your old guff."

"Supposing she doesn't come back," Elsie had started to say, but he didn't want to hear it and he jumped off the step and joined his brothers who had gathered to grin at his discomfiture. Elsie watched them, a few thrusts of fists, a few raised voices, another soothing voice and they climbed into Danny's van and drove away.

One of the pickers stopped by her window, his sack full of bits of copper and aluminium, the wheel of a bicycle hanging like a huge medallion down his back.

"You've got a bold one there," he said. "And to look at her you'd think butter wouldn't melt in her mouth, cross eyes and all. Have they gone to fetch her?"

"Gone to Old Mac's," Hannah joined in, leaning her large behind against the caravan, looking the picker up and down. "Did you get much today? That's a miserable old wheel you got. I'll take it off your hands for 50p."

"Go back to your knitting, old woman," he said scornfully. "I have a buyer for this. A proper bicycle dealer."

"Well that shifted him," Hannah said, as he heaved his load up on his bicycle and wobbled away down the road, disappearing like a ghost in the fog of burning plastic bags and litter. "Poking his nose in where he isn't wanted. I hope you told him nothing."

Elsie turned her face to the wall and groaned. "Hurts you, does it?" Hannah asked. "You shouldn't have left that black doctor put the wire in. I wouldn't let a black doctor next or near me. Nor one of them women doctors either. But you were always the one with notions. I'll go away now and look after your poor childer for you. They're crying with the hunger, I expect, if they're not watching the telly."

The blessed peace when she had gone flowed over Elsie, better than any pain killer. The second pony munched near her window, stretched the full length of his tether. Brigid could have fallen off by now. She could be lying on the road with a broken arm or leg. In the distance the siren of an ambulance screamed hysterically. That's probably her, Elsie thought. They have picked her broken little body up and brought her to hospital. She's unconscious or maybe dead. I'll never see her again.

The dark closed in on the caravan. Elsie listened for the voices of her children as they made their different ways to their aunts" caravans. If Brigid were here she would come and say goodnight to her. She would cuddle up against her and she would not push her away impatiently. "Brigid, Brigid," she groaned aloud.

"I'm here Mama," Brigid was beside her, hopping up and down on the bed. "Did you see me? I never fell off once. Did Dada see me?"

Exasperation filled every inch of Elsie's body. It took charge of the pain. She wanted to sit up and shake Brigid till her teeth rattled. She opened her mouth to say, "your father'll kill you and good enough for you," when Brigid said, "I wouldn't have done it if he hadn't turned orange. The sun turned him orange and I wanted to ride him while he was that colour."

"He wasn't that colour at all," Elsie said. "You only thought he was that colour."

"He was. I saw him," Brigid insisted, her crossed eyes glinting with temper. "Can I cuddle into you Mama? Can I sleep here with you?" What was the use of anything, thought Elsie. The child was safe and sound and wanting to sleep beside her and she didn't want anyone in the bed with her. She wanted to toss and turn and groan in privacy.

"I might keep you awake."

"You won't, Mama. And I'll get you anything you want. Will I make you a sup of tay? Did the fellas see me? What did they say?"

Elsie began to laugh. "Oh my God," she groaned. "Don't make me laugh. My jaw aches. They were raging. They'll kill you when they get their hands on you."

"I don't care," Brigid said. "It was worth it. I'll kick them and I'll ride the pony again and again. I've him tethered now. I fell off loads of times but I got up again. It's easy. I'll practise. If they see I'm good, they'll let me do it. I'm not like you, Mama. I'm like my Dada and no one will bate me into the ground. You shouldn't let Dada hit you."

Oh Mary, Mother of God intercede for me at the throne of mercy, prayed Elsie silently. Give me patience. Help me to say the right thing. She said nothing. She thought of the money wrapped tightly under the stone, waiting to liberate her.

Brigid was almost asleep. She flung an arm across Elsie's stomach and said "I'll make money for you when I'm big and you'll be able to buy anything you like."

"Won't you want to buy things for yourself, maybe your own pony?"

"When I'm big I won't care about the pony," Brigid said. "When I'm big." She was already asleep. Elsie looked down at her pale freckled skin and carroty eyelashes and she smiled. An orange sun and an orange horse and orange hair. She looked with love at Brigid and she understood her world. For a moment she had a glimpse of some meaning beyond the caravan and the dump and the pile of money buried under the bank. Was it heaven that she was thinking about? Some place up there, way beyond the sky, where you could go to bed and rest easy, a place like the Dallas of the telly without the fighting and arguing. All the arguing would wear you out. You either got worn out or as fat as a pig, like some of her sisters-in-law who stuffed themselves even when they weren't hungry. It was the opposite with her. Her stomach couldn't take food when the arguing and shouting was going on. After a beating she couldn't eat for weeks.

An orange horse was like a flame, she thought. It would burn the air up as it raced by your window. It would warm your heart but never singe your soul. It could fly up to the clouds and down again. It could give you more notions than anyone would ever know. You could touch it and not feel it. You could feel it and not touch it. It could have a meaning that you might never understand but knowing it was there would change your life. It would help you find a way to spend the money you saved. It would save your life if you let it. It would make your jaw ache less. It was better than the holy nun, God forgive her for thinking such a thing. If Margaret Anne had seen it she might never have choked on her own vomit. An orange horse that never was could be the greatest secret of all. She stroked Brigid's hair and fell asleep.

People in the town said afterwards that the flames of the fire turned the sky the maddest orange they had ever seen. Three of the caravans went up together but the only casualties were a mother and daughter. Their caravan went up first. The heat was so intense it was a wonder the whole lot of them didn't go up. A gas cylinder exploded. The police were questioning a man who had thrown a can of petrol into the first caravan and set it alight. He was drunk. He didn't know what he was doing. There were screams from the caravan, terrible screams that those who heard them would never forget. But the firemen found nothing. It was the heat, they said. It was an incinerator. A Hiachi van was burned and left a carcass of twisted metal. A pony died and left a charred body but in the caravan there was nothing. Nothing.

Rita Ann Higgins

Witch In the Bushes
(for Padraic Fiacc)

I know a man
who tried
to eat a rock
a big rock
grey and hard,
unfriendly too.

Days later
he is still grinding,
the rock
is not getting
any smaller.
Because of this
rock in the jaw,
this impediment,
the man has become
even more angry.

No one
could look at him,
but a few
hard cases did.
They were mostly dockers;
they reckoned,

"We have seen
the savage seas
rise over our dreams,
we can look
at a bull-head
eating a rock'.

The years passed
slowly and painfully,
until one day
the rock was no more,
neither was much of the man.

He didn't
grind the rock down,
the rock
hammered a job
on him and his ego.

Then, one day
an old woman
came out of the bushes
wearing a black patch
and a questionnaire,
in her wand hand
she held a posh red pencil,
well pared.

She questioned him
between wheezes
(she had emphysema
from smoking damp tobacco
and inhaling fumes
from her open fire
in the woods)
if all that anger
for all those years
was worth it.

Old Rockie Jaw
couldn't answer
he had forgotten
the reason
and the cause.

He concluded,
"Anger is ok
if you spill it,
but chewing
is assuredly
murder on the teeth.'

He had learned
his lesson
he would
pull himself together
smarten up like,
turn the other cheek,
he would go easy
on the oils that aged him.

Every now and then
he weakened,
he let the voice
from the rock take over,
an army voice
with a militant tone,

"A man is a man
and a real man
must spit feathers
when the occasion arises.'

Like all good voices
this one
had an uncle,
it was the voice
of the uncle
that bothered him,
it always
had the same warning,

"About
the witch in the bushes,"

it said,
"Watch her,
she never sleeps".

Woman's Inhumanity To Woman
(Galway Labour Exchange)

And in this cage ladies and gentlemen,
we have the powers that be.

Powder power,
lipstick power,
pencil power,
paper power,
cigarette in the left hand power,
raised right of centre half plucked eyebrow, Cyclops power,
big tits power,
piercing eyes power,
filed witches nails power,
I own this building power,
I own you power,
fear of the priest power,
fear of the Black n'Tans power.

Your father drank too much power,
your sister had a baby when she was fifteen power,
where were you last night power,
upstairs in your house is dirty power,
the state of your hotpress power,
the state of your soul power,
keep door closed power,
keep eyes closed power,
no smoking power,
money for the black babies power,
queue only here power,
sign only there power,
breathe only when I tell you power.

No pissing on the staff power,
jingle of keys power,
your brother signs and works power,
ye have a retarded child power,
you sign and work power,
look over your shoulder power,
look over your brother's shoulder power,
I know your mother's maiden name power,
look at the ground power,
I know your father's maiden name power,

spy in the sky power,
spy in the toilet power,
fart in front of a bishop power.

Apologise for your mother's colour hair power,
apologise for your father's maiden name power,
apologise for being born power.

Some People
(for Eoin)

Some people know what it is like,

to be called a cunt in front of their children
to be short for the rent
to be short for the light
to be short for school books
to wait in Community Welfare waiting rooms full of smoke
to wait two years to have a tooth looked at
to wait another two years to have a tooth out (the same tooth)
to be half strangled by your varicose veins, but you're 198th on
the list
to talk into a banana on a jobsearch scheme
to talk into a banana in a jobsearch dream
to be out of work
to be out of money
to be out of fashion
to be out of friend
to be in for the Vincent de Paul man
to be in space for the milk man
(sorry, mammy isn't in today she's gone to Mars for the
weekend)
to be in Puerto Rico this week for the blanket man
to be in Puerto Rico next week for the blanket man
to be dead for the coal man
(sorry, mammy passed away in her sleep, overdose of coal in the
teapot)
to be in hospital unconscious for the rent man (St Judes ward 4th
floor)
to be second hand
to be second class
to be no class
to be looked down on
to be walked on
to be pissed on
to be shat on

and other people don't.

Máire Mhac an tSaoi

Tarlachaint

Bhí timpeall na cille á thabhairt agam,
Tré phóirsí an fhothraigh seo inchinne agam,
Cogarnaíl fheoite im'chluasa,
Siosarnach gainní fúm ag gluaiseacht,
Mé ag meabhrú ar phaidrín na gcloch
Ó áirse stuaiceach go háirse
I gcoim ulaidh mo phlaicide,
Nuair thaibhsigh chugham go hobann,
De léargas reatha idir mé agus léas,
An neach:
Ard, álainn, caoldubh, lúbach,
Beoldearg, aolchneas, rúnda,
Mallaithe,
Gan gnéas,
Mar a bheadh *soutane* á chaitheamh aige
Agus gothaí an rinnce air —
Cén fáth go gceapaim
Go bhfuil cúr lásaí agus fronsaí cheáimric
'Na gcóta cabhlach ag coipeadh
Fé iamh na n-iliomad cnaipe sin?

A Happening

I was doing the stations of the graveyard/Through the porches
of my crumbling brain,/A withered whispering in my ears,/A
hissing of sand moving under me,/Meditating on the stones of
my rosary/From pointed arch to arch/Within the charnel
enclosure of my skull,/When there appeared to me suddenly,/
Fleetingly in silhouette,/A being:/Tall, beautiful, dark and
slender, sinuous,/Red-lipped, lime-white, secret, /Perverse,/
Sexless,/Wearing, as it might be, a *soutane*,/And striking a
dancing attitude —/Why is it that I think/There is a foam of
laces and cambric flounces,/A frothing petticoat,/Under that
multiplicity of buttons?

(*Trans. Máire Mhac an tSaoi*)

I Leith Na Ruaidhe

Rabharta rua na hInide,
  Roide i mbéal na trá,
Is an buinne fola fém' easna
  Ní móide dhó an lán ...

Rua fós an luifearnach
  I mboireann an gharraí,
Rua ceannacha an Mhárta,
  Rua níochán do-ním ...

Trua an mhoill seo an Earraigh,
  Rua gach radharc im dháil,
Aiséirí rua is aifreann
  Is éadach rua um Cháisc!

Reddish

The russet springs of Shrove,/Red mud at the mouth of the bay,/And the haemorrhage under my rib/Not likely to reach full-tide...

Russet the growth of weed/In the burren of the yard,/Russet the face of March,/Russet the wash I launder ...

Pity this Spring delaying,/Russet all sights around,/Red mass and resurrection,/For Easter russet raiment.

(Trans. Máire Mhac an tSaoi)

Cearca

i

Is cuimhin liom beinn dá gúna
    idir mé agus na cearca:
Triantán dorcha éadaigh
    Mar a bheadh seol naomhóige,
Agus an pointe socair sa chosmas
    Gur mise é
Ag gliúcaíl dá dhroim
    Im portán sceimhlithe.

Ní bhíonn an bríd sin de chearca ruadhearga
    Acu, a thuilleadh:
Cearca chomh mór le muca,
    Caora tine acu in áit na súl,
Goib chorránacha, neamhthruamhéileacha orthu,
    Agus camachrúba fúthu,
Innealta chun mé 'stolladh —
    Ní fheicim timpeall iad níos mó.

Bhí buataisí leis sa phictiúir
    Agus aprún garbh,
Ach caithim ailtireacht a dh'imirt orthusan
    Ar bhonn prionsabail,
Ní ritheann siad chugham
    Dá ndeoin —
"Ní cuimhin leat," deir daoine, "Do sheanamháthair."
    Is cuimhin, ón gcromán anuas.

ii

I Saloinice, ina dhíbeartach,
    Saolaíodh an garsúinín;
Banfhlaith de phór *Tatarin*
    Ba mháthair dó:
Bean choinleachta 'bea í tráth
    I gcomplacht an Tsarina,
I gcúirt na mbuibhsíe liúidí,
    I gcúirt na réamhdhaoine.

Throid 'athair le Deniken sa Iúcráin,
    Lean teideal captaein dó;
Críocha Gréag níor óir dó
    Mar altram don aoinghin:
Lofacht is stair na Meánmhara bréine
    Mhúch air an t-aer ann;
Tháinig 'na 'reachtaire cearc' go Cuileann,
    Cuileann an fhuachta, *Cold Collon*, in Éirinn.

Does nobody here speak Greek?
    Ars' an leanbh,
I mBéarla crochta na n-uasal
    Dár díobh é,
Ach lonnaigh 'na dhiaidh sin go sásta ar an bhfód,
    Is, nuair a théadh dian air
Searmanas nósmhar an teaghlaigh,
    Dhein sé a ghearán leis na cearca!

Fiabhras a d'ídigh é
    Fiabhras dóibh siúd
Ba bhreith báis ar óige
    Roimh *phenicillin;*
Oidhre na machairí résteipe anoir
    Síneadh i reilig os Bóinn
Eaglais na hÉireann níor cheadaigh
    Cros an Phápaire ar an uaigh.

iii

Ní maith liom cearca —
    Bíonn boladh agus bús uathu —
Ach is maith liom an dá scéilín sin,
    Agus is ar chearca a bhraitheann siad.

Hens

i

I remember a fold of her skirt/Between me and the hens:/A
dark triangle of stuff/Like the sail on a currach,/And that fixed
point in the cosmos,/Which was me,/Peering over it,/A panic-
stricken crab.

They don't have that breed of russet hen/Any more:/Hens as
big as pigs/With burning coals for eyes,/And sickle-like, pitiless
beaks,/Standing on crooked claws,/Arrayed to tear me
apart—/ I don't see them around nowadays.

There were boots in the picture too/And a rough apron,/But I
have to reconstruct those/From first principles,/They don't
come to me/Of their own accord .../"You don't," people say,
"Remember your grandmother."/I do, from the hips down.

ii

In Salonica, an exile,/The little boy was born,/His mother a
princess/Of Tatarin's race,/Once a lady-in-waiting/In the train
of the Tsarina,/At the court of the *Bwivshige lyudy*,/The former
people.

His father had fought with Danikin, in the Ukraine,/And kept
his captain's title;/He did not hold with Greece/As a foster-
home for their only one:/The corruption and history of the
stinking Mediterranean/Stifled its air for him;/He came, as a
poultry-steward, to Collon,/Cold Collon, in Ireland

"Does nobody here speak Greek?"/Said the child,/In the stilted
English of that nobility/To which he belonged,/But later he
settled contentedly there,/And, when the established
ceremony/Of the household became too much for him,/He
made his complaint to the hens!

It was a fever that finished him:/One of those fevers/That
sentenced the young to death/Before penicillin;/The heir to the
Eastern plains of the level steppe/Is buried North of the
Boyne;/The Church of Ireland forbade/A popish cross on his
grave.

iii

I don't like hens —/They are smelly and fussy —/But I like those two little stories,/And both are dependent on hens.

(Trans. Máire Mhac an tSaoi)

Clairr O' Connor

For The Time Being

I grew up with ghosts. They hung on walls between the pictures of the saints. Relatives everywhere. Great grandparents and cousins of several generations were recalled as if they had just stepped out for a walk and were due back for supper that night. Only the past and future mattered in our house. The present was not important. My parents gave the impression that the present was a gauzy, insubstantial thing. People who lived there, they implied, were somehow lightweight. By seven years old, I knew the daily trivia of two generations back. When granduncle Will lost his pipe, what colour stockings great aunt May wore on Sundays. Who fainted at aunt Bella's wedding. Why the catholic faith was the only one fit to prepare civilised people for death. The fun of past pilgrimages and retreats. Why grasping at the here and now was an offence in the eyes of God.

This was difficult for a child, the present being the only thing that could matter to one so young. When I revelled in some achievement or sank under small disasters, I was told that in the long run it wouldn't matter.

I articulated my rage through screaming fits or sullen silences, to remind myself and others that I inhabited the here and now. I was told I was a cross child. I'm sure I was unbearable. Other children were urged on in the game of life, "get out there and compete". But Sunday recreation in our house after mass and dinner mostly consisted of visiting graveyards and admiring or deploring the state they were in. Stonework and types of lettering were given detailed scrutiny. Photographs were taken of the happy family perched on tombs. Other people seemed to go to the sea for the day or pick blackberries, depending on season, but we picked over the bones of relatives or had fierce arguments about who to leave out of the family album.

I saw my first dead person when I was four years old. An ancient relative, she was laid out in white and clasped an outsized rosary. I wondered how she could have been so well prepared. Funerals were a treat, you see, none too young to enjoy them. My father worked in the local morgue. Preparing bodies for their eternal journey was an everyday event. Other children were given tours of their daddy's office or shop. But, even as a toddler, I was a regular visitor at the morgue. Once, while playing with my dolls underneath a sheeted table, I pulled the cover off to make a new outfit for one of them. A cold man was presumably colder for my assumptions. When Daddy and his colleagues found me, they chortled in appreciation.

Later on, in college, when my best friend's grandmother died, she fainted at the funeral. No years of practice behind her, her legs simply gave way. But to get back to this difficulty with living in the present. I have always envied those normal adults who apparently go through life sequentially neither dawdling over the past or imagining a future that may not happen. Reflection and regret have dogged my steps since childhood. I reflect too often and regret too much. Inactivity takes over in the form of a very active nostalgia for something so intangible that it cannot be named or guessed at.

Time passes. I invariably get very little done. My numerous diaries lie half-filled at year's end, while my list notebooks expand and sometimes explode with resolutions and good intentions. My mind goes in several directions at once but to no purpose.

All of this started way back of course, and maybe if I was made of sterner stuff or had above average talent at anything it wouldn't matter so much. In junior school when I was five, I was picked to play a witch in a hallowe'en play. I thought of nothing else for weeks. The present was suddenly overwhelmingly important. I had put together an old dressing gown and made a makeshift broom. My mother made my witch's hat. I practised for hours. Walking, grimacing, twirling in my outfit, I paraded in front of the hall mirror and congratulated myself ahead of the event. The great night came. All the family, mother, father, sister, brother, aunts and uncles had been pressganged to attend.

A half an hour before we were to set out for the school stage, the phone rang. Somebody had died. I cannot be more specific. To this day, I do not know who, in fact, died. It was a second cousin once removed. The name meant nothing. Yet, it changed everything. My father said he'd have to go to the church. I howled. When that got me nowhere, I kicked in the glass door of the china cabinet. Glass sprayed the general area. Little spears of it, lilliputian parts were picked off various family members. My mother screamed, then, realising I was safe, slapped me soundly. Glasses that had been too good to use except after funerals scattered the floor, shattered forever. The first aid box was produced. Elaborate plasters were applied after a thorough disinfection. The survivors were less than enthusiastic about my stage debut. In the end, my mother and sister came. The rest stayed at home or more probably stole off to the familiar pleasures of a funeral.

Enraged by desertion, I gave the performance of my young life and was rewarded by a box of chocolates from the teacher. I scoffed the lot backstage even before my make-up was removed. I could not bear to share with traitors or lukewarm supporters. Having contained myself on the return journey, I threw up in the front hall at home. I suspected from then on that present glory was stained by that journey every one of us must take. Years later, in drama school, I appalled my class mates when, asked to improvise a happy scene from childhood, I enacted the burial service. Latin bits and all. While admiring my feat of memory they couldn't ignore my seeming callousness. To this day, it is the parts I do not get that worry me the most. Second in line are the parts I might get. The ones I'm playing are a hallway, to be passed through, for after all, the present is just a moment, isn't it?

To get back to childhood. I don't think I was allowed a childhood until my late twenties, when I had some time and some spare money. On my twenty-sixth birthday, I ran amok in toy shops buying up all the silly stuffed toys, train sets and magic potions I could lay my hands on. I had just finished a long run in a soap opera and the cash flow was good. I said I was buying for nieces and nephews. The sales assistants had recognised me from the TV. I had woken up that very morning thinking about the time cousin Nat had taken my teddy. I was fourteen.

He was a toddler. He was visiting. When he was leaving, I pulled my teddy from him.

"It's mine," he yelled.

"No. It's mine," I snapped.

"Don't be silly," my mother's voice intoned levelly, "I gave it to Nat. You don't need it anymore."

"I do," I squeezed through clenched teeth, "he's mine."

But Nat knew he was on a winner when I pinched him to loosen his grip. At twenty six, I bought the biggest teddy in the shop. He dwarfs my Beatrix Potter collection but I love him best of all. Dear Pad.

Pilgrimages were a big treat in our family. While my peers were girl guides and scouts, my siblings and I scaled Croagh Patrick and dented our knees in Lough Derg, asking forgiveness for sins and other follies that we'd neither the experience or the opportunity to commit. I protested vehemently at this rigid orthodoxy and said I'd prefer an outing to the circus or carnival. This was taken as a sign of worldliness and to this day, in my family, though I'm by far the most financially insecure, being an actress, I'm regarded as the one who is most obsessed with money.

But all of us, Tim, my brother and Ginny, my sister and myself have had to react against my parents' philosophy, that this world is just the passage way to the next. Otherwise, one supposes that we'd have given up after mastering the crawl. Tim, I think, is the one who has made most profit from his childhood experiences. Clever and opportunistic, he won a scholarship to college and managed to stay out of debt as an undergraduate. The only one I ever knew who managed that feat. During summer holidays he went to America and worked in mortuaries there. He came back at the end of each holiday with the fascinating details of how death was dealt with, the other side of the Atlantic. My father was enthralled. Five years after college, Tim was a partner in the local funeral home. In another two, he had installed cousin Phil to look after his interests there and winged his way back to America. Now he owns a string of Gardens of Rest for the pets of the rich. Fifi and Scottie have their own little plots and headstones. Their owners can weep over them whenever they please. Tim is the success of the family. On his last visit home, he bought our parents a grave extension. He thought the family plot was a bit overcrowded, so he extended it to twice its size. Daddy was really pleased. "Great-aunt May will have a larger crowd than she expected."

At the end of his stay, Tim hired a Rover and drove the parents to view the country's better graveyards. They stayed in grade A hotels and came back more refreshed than others who had spent a month in the sun. Daddy's retired now but he can indulge his professional interest by keeping an eye on Cousin Phil. In fact, his funeral attendances have gathered pace over the years. Some of his age group die regularly now. He's no longer removed from death by a generation. A mixed pleasure.

My sister Ginny, in a triumphant attempt to banish the present totally and to outshine Tim, joined a contemplative silent order of nuns in France. There was a festive family party before her departure. Cakes, candles, fireworks, photos, the lot. Three generations turned out to it. Aunt Bella said black had always suited Ginny and that she'd be the best looking nun in the order. Ginny was beautiful in the excitement of it all. I got drunk on too much gin and too little tonic and begged her to change her mind. Uncle Mike called me a show-off and a troublemaker.

Ginny spent five years in France, only speaking when allowed. She was given extra space in the family album and her photo in her nun's habit stood right next to Tim's on the piano. When she left the order and ran off with a jesuit priest, it played havoc with all that. Down came the piano picture and my mother locked away that particular album in a special drawer. Tim and myself were the only family at her wedding in New York. She lives there now with her husband and two children. As she says herself, she's a *now* person. She spent the first thirty years of her life trying to make sense of her past and preparing for death, so she needs to spend time in the present. We indulge in transatlantic calls when we're most broke, guiltily defying thrift like children in a sweet shop.

But to get back to me. I married Richard, my English tutor in college, as soon as I graduated. Nobody wanted me to do that, which is why, I think, I did it. He was fifty years old with two adult children and a dead wife behind him. I think it was the dead wife that attracted me the most, to tell you the truth. At this stage, I was attempting a truce with family ghosts, catholicity and the family's passion for funerals. Logically, the family should have been pleased by my choice but nature doesn't hold with logic most of the time. It didn't last of course, not their hostility, but the marriage.

Three years into it, I realised I was living with a grandfather, but the duties were more demanding. In company, I was delighted when people took us for father and daughter. I teased Richard about it. At home, I got fed up having to help organise his manuscripts, a task I had revelled in as acolyte. Proof-reading a book on 19th century Romanticism finally ended it for me. I realised I was postponing adventure in the present for a sickly nostalgia with the past and an ordered future that would soon descend into cocoa and early bedtimes. I left like a coward, in the night, one suitcase in hand and a short note on the breakfast tray. He deserved better but my courage was limited.

From now on, I told myself, I'll do something that's worthwhile and rooted in the present. After three years playing child-bride, nursemaid and secretary, I wasn't feeling very confident. Determination grew once I'd settled into a two-roomed flat and I'd managed to survive the first week without too much trauma. I made lists. What would become of me? Astronaut, too tied to the future. Bank manager, the handicap of innumeracy. Bookshop owner, idealistic but no capital to invest. Artist, no talent.

I woke one night to the nightmare sweat of shattered glass and spewed chocolate, a witch beating a coffin. My stage debut came back like forbidden fruit. I would become an actress. A late starter at drama school, twenty five among the teenagers, I felt strained and nervous at first, not least because I had to work nights in a restaurant to make ends meet. But small successes gave me courage and I realised within six months that I had made the right choice. The opportunity to live many lives in the parts I played was a perfect testing ground for my resolution to live in the present. Insecure at the best of times, the actress is only as good as her last part. Getting and holding parts would demand daily effort.

-And it worked like that for a few years. I felt I was laying the family ghosts finally. I was inhabiting the present. The past could forget itself and the future could remain unformed until it arrived. Doubts came quite unexpectedly, in the middle of a post production party. The play was *Doll's House.* I had played Nora to full houses. I put down my wine glass and fled the party. I began to feel I wasn't living in the present at all. I was playing the parts well because I knew they were merely parts. I was evading the sum of the whole, just as I had run from home to marriage, from marriage to stage.

Time had passed. That couldn't be ignored. The last six months, I had shuffled from my soap opera in the studio by day to Nora on stage at night. I had felt stretched and alive. Was this living in the present though? Twenty six was staring me in the face. That's when I knew I had to get right back to it. Childhood, I mean. Not on the psychiatrist's chair but to the very activities that had been cut short. The toy spree took care of some of it. Always a listmaker, I made hectic lists now. Aimed at resolving once and for all the feeling I had, that my parents had robbed me of a childhood. Not through neglect or cruelty but simply by their insistence, that in this life we are merely passing through on the way to the other side.

Making lists cleared my head. All the childhood funerals merged into one ghastly parody of a life holding its breath for the final curtain, having skipped all actors, not to mention the interval. My twenty-sixth birthday would make up for all that. Birthdays were not celebrated in our house, not the ones of the living anyway. I had the misfortune to share a birthday with grand-uncle Will. Dead before I had arrived, nevertheless, his photo framed my birthdays.

"Poor old uncle Will, he would be a hundred and two today if the Lord had spared him," Daddy would remark mournfully into his tea cup.

"But I'm sixteen today," I'd protest.

"True enough," he'd rejoin, "and you're one year nearer to

where uncle Will is."

I often wonder if one of the reasons I rushed into marriage with an older man was possibly the influence of grand-uncle Will's photograph. He was missed on my birthdays and Richard, my husband had an expansive moustache just like his. Anyway, on with my list.

To break the bind of catholic orthodoxy my parents embraced, I resolved on several things. The first being, to eat meat only on Fridays. Big steaks preferably. Friday had always been a fish day in my childhood home. Next, I decided to go to mass when I felt like it, but never on a Sunday. I resolved absolutely, not to attend funerals except those of close friends. Should be safe on that one for a few years anyway.

These resolutions worked in their own way, at least for a while. But the day came when I realised that the deritualisation of my parents' rituals had, in themselves become rituals. Their observation pushed me in the opposite direction merely. New lists were necessary. I understood this when my local butcher didn't have any steak left on Friday night and I left his shop redfaced and crying. My misery at that present moment was rooted in fish Fridays.

But it was when I was gorging boxes of chocolates during Lent just for the hell of it, that I knew things were far gone. The present is a natural sequence to the past for most people. They don't have to use reverse ritual to try and convince themselves of their adulthood. After the gorge came austerity. To outdo the ascetics became a new goal. Frugality and restraint mastered me for a time. I lost two stone and played Peter Pan in panto on a three month run. I felt I was a child for the first time in my life, the eternal child, in fact.

After the show, when others were tucked into pizzas, I sipped my coffee and munched salad, crunching my carrots with happiness. I made personal appearances opening toyshops, children's clothes shops and loved it all. The family came to see me fly through air. Daddy said, "A bit dangerous, isn't it? I hope you've got proper insurance."

Tim came backstage on one of his trips home. He thought I was terrific and slipped me a hefty cheque to prove it. His business was expanding. He was excited about the possibilities of a dry-freeze method of storing the bodies of pets and humans at the precise moment of death. At some future date, when scientific research caught up, the bodies could be brought back to life. So, it had finally happened. In a little while, death would be cancelled altogether. The future would stretch out indefinitely. As well as the family mortgage, all the average young couple had to do was take out financial cover for a family freeze compartment to secure togetherness beyond the last breath. I couldn't eat for several days, not even a carrot.

Not even a carrot! True. Tim had surpassed himself. While he'd been beating the future, I remained mired in doubt. I'd run the gamut from gorge to abstinence on the see-saw between past and future, the present somehow escaping. Then I saw my mistake. I had assumed the present was happening to other people elsewhere while the memories of shattered glass, spewed chocolate and final rites speared me to the past. But maybe they were precisely the things that catapulted me forward? Not a fast forward, but forward nevertheless. Just then, the telephone rang. It was Richard. He was ringing to say it was our tenth anniversary. I said, how could that be if I'd fled the marital tomb seven years ago? I hung up and decided to get an answering machine as an early birthday present.

Paula Meehan

Elegy For a Child

It is not that the spring brings
You back. Birds riotous about
The house, fledglings learn to fly.

Nor that coming on petals drifted in the orchard
Is like opening your door, a draught of pastel,
A magpie hoard of useless bright.

Clouds move over the river
Under the sun — a cotton sheet shook out.
The pines bring me news
From deeper in the woods:
The rain will come sing on the roof soon.

It is not the day's work in the garden,
The seedlings neatly leaf mould mulched in lines.
Not the woodpile trim bespeaking good husbandry
And conjuring up the might-have-been.

It is not the anarchic stream
In a stone sucking dash past the crane's haunt, fickle,
Sky mirror now, now shattered bauble,

Nor the knowledge of planets in proper orbit,
Their passage through my fourth house
Fixed before I was born.
It is not that the night you died
A star plummeted to earth.
It is not that I watched it fall.

It is not that I was your mother,
Nor the rooted deep down loss,
That has brought me this moment
To sit by the window and weep.

You were but a small bird ready
Within me, balanced for flight.

Don't Speak To Me Of Martyrs

Up there on the platform a man
speaks of the people: of what
we need, of who we really are, of how
we must fight to liberate ourselves.

Down through the cigarette smoke
the high windows cast
ecstatic light to the floorboards
stiletto pocked and butt scorched

but now such golden pools of sun to bask in there.
I am fish,
water my demesne.
The room pulses in, then out of focus

and all this talk of armalite and ballot box
is robbed of meaning, becomes
sub-melody, sonic undertow,
a room of children chanting off

by heart a verse. I'm nine or ten,
the Central Model School,
Miss Shannon beats out the metre
 with her stick.

I wind up in the ghost place
the language rocks me to,
a cobwebby state, chilled vault
littered with our totems;

a tattered Plough and Stars,
a bloodstained Proclamation,
Connolly strapped wounded to a chair,
Mayblossom in Inchicore.

I am following my father's steps
on a rainy Sunday in the National Museum,
by talisman of torc, carved spiral,
Sile na Gig's yoni made luscious in stone.

And somewhere there is vestige
of my mother nursing me to sleep,
when all my world was touch,
when all my world was peace.

And in there too a September evening
the Pro-Cathedral, girls in rows at prayer,
gaze at the monstrance, lulled to adoration,
mesmeric in frankincense and candlelight:

"Hail our life our sweetness and our hope
To thee do we cry poor banished children of Eve
To thee do we send up our sighs
Mourning and weeping in this valley of tears"

I push back to the surface, break clear,
the light has come on, fluorescent,
and banishes my dreaming self.
It is after all an ordinary room.

And we are ordinary people.
We pull our collars up and head
for the new moon sky of our city
fondling each whorled bead in our macabre rosaries.

Don't speak to me of Stephen the Martyr
the host snug in his palm
slipping through the wounded streets
to keep his secret safe.

Deirdre Brennan

An Tobar

Mise an eilit faoi dhraoícht
éirithe as an leaba dhearg
Talamh uisciúil faoi mo chrúba.
San idirsholas cloisim
Sioscaireacht an tobair
Mar a shásófaí mo thart.

Cailín órga an tobair mé,
Ban-draoi uaigneach na hoíche
Tagtha ón duibheagán gan ghrinneall,
An finscéal i gcroí-gach fir.
Meallaim chugam iad
Go sásófaí mo thart.

Mise an páiste cosnochta,
Poipíní feoite im' ghruaig
A thagann le buicéad cruanta
Chun uisce a tharraingt.
Frog ar leac in áilleacht ghréine,
Tá mo phrionsa ann romham.

Mise an file dobrónach
Ag fánadóireacht ar bhruach,
A glaodh chun an tobair
Go mblaisfinn óm' bhoiseog
Ceol do bheochta ar theanga
Agus bíog do shacraiminte i mo bhéal.

The Well

I am the enchanted hind/Who breaks cover/Wet ground under
my hooves,/In the half light I hear/The whispering of the
well/Where my thirst might be slaked.

I am the golden girl of the well/The lonely sorceress of
night/Come from the bottomless deep/The legend in men's
hearts./I lure them to me/That my thirst may be satisfied.

I am the barefooted child/Wilted poppies in my hair/Who
comes with an enamel bucket/To draw water./A frog in the
glory of sunlight on a stone,/My prince there before me!

I am the languid poet/Loitering on its brink/Who was called to
the well/That I might taste from cupped hands/The music of
your vitality/On my tongue/And the pulse of your
sacrament/In my mouth.

(Trans. Deirdre Brennan and Máirín Ní Dhonnchadha)

Dealbhóireacht
(*"Of Ancient Seas"* — *John Behan* — *Polychrome Steel*)

Aistear na gcianta eadrainn beirt
Mise agus taibhse mo thosaigh,
Ach cailltear fós mé
I bhfoilmhe a shúile
I gcraos a bhéil;
San fholús ainaithnid úd
A chuir ag gabháil
Cuisle bhriste an tsaoil.

Cá mhinice a bhuail mé leis
In aigéan m'intinne
I liath-ghlaiseacht uisce,
Mar fheamainn ghaoithe
Ag sileadh de tharm
Go doimhneacht duibheagáin!
Nó ag snámh trí mo chorp
Go mothaím ar chraiceann
Sleanntaigh mo chuid feola
Ag titim ó chéile,
Is mar shliogáin ag tuirlingt
Go grinneall ársa mo chuimhne.

Sculpture
(*"Of Ancient Seas"* — *John Behan* — *Polychrome Steel*)

The drift of ages between us/Me and the ghost of my
beginning,/But still I lose myself/In the emptiness of his
eyes/In the hunger of his mouth;/In that unfathomable
void/That set beating/The feeble pulse of life.

How often have I met him/In the ocean of my mind/In the
grey-greenness of water,/Like tattered seaweed/Streaming past
me/To bottomless depths./Or swimming through my
body/Until I feel on my skin/The scales of flesh shatter/And
plummet like shells/To the ancient bed of memory.

(*Trans. Deirdre Brennan and Máirín Ní Dhonnchadha*)

Scothanna geala

Nár mhothaigh an geimhreadh riamh
Is beag acu gaoth ná báisteach
Ar fhuinneog an tsamhraidh shíoraí.

Priomúil ina bprócaí faoi bhláth
Ag amharc uathu amach
Niamhracht a loinnir
Ag fionnadh im' thimpeall.

Blianta neamhshuntasacha ag imeacht
Fáiscthe i ngréasán fréamha,
Na séasúir ar seachrán
I dtais chúngracht fionn mhóna

Cathain a bhrisfidh mé
Prócaí mo cheangaltais?
Seasfaidh mé anseo
Go gciorclóidh féar mé

Diúlfaidh mé an bháisteach
A rachaidh i ndísc ionam
Go bpéacfadh nóiníní móra samhrata
ó shílcheapach mo chroí

Caithfidh mé amach piotail mo chuid gruaige
I ngach gaoth a shéideann
Agus i gcré oighreata geimhridh
Clúdóidh mé síolta m'aiséirí.

Bright Blossoms

Bright blossoms/That never felt winter/Little do they care
about wind and rain/In the window of eternal summer.

Primulas flowering in their pots/Look around them/The sheen
of their light/Mellowing

The worthless years pass/Compressed in a web of roots/The
seasons gone astray/In the damp press of peat.

When will I break/My binding pots?/I will stand here/Until
grass encircles me.

I will suck the rain/That will run dry in me/Until great summer
daisies sprout/From the seedbed of my heart.

I will toss out the petals of my hair/In every wind that
blows/And in icy winter clay/I will cover resurrection seeds.

(Trans. Deirdre Brennan and Máirín Ní Dhonnchadha)

Dolores Walsh

East of Ireland

It is two weeks since I heard, yet still I am confounded by it. Rhein does not know. But I must tell him soon. I delay only because I know what his reaction will be.

"Get rid of it," he will say, in the same tone he uses every time there is a mess. Like that time he used a spade on the beech marten which had nested in the attic, causing us longer nights.

Today is market day in Alkmaar and I have gone to shop among the stalls. For the first time, Hans of the cheeses cannot tempt me with the subtleties of taste between the ageing Goudas. Although it is Spring, the tourists have not yet descended for the ritual parading of produce before the stalls burst into action.

I have bought raw herring for Rhein. Pickled in brine. In the glass it floats, dead and grey. Like a foetus. It is in this moment standing at the fish stall that I decide: this moment when my eye wanders from the herring to the eels burrowing in the crushed ice; I will tell him tonight. I watch the fishmonger select a sinewy black body from the marble slab and hold it out like a ruler to the woman before him.

"Nice. Will it feed three of us, do you think?" she asks him in Dutch. It twists, sunlight glancing off the glistening skin. "Ja, seker. He is good and fat." The man holds the knife poised. At a nod from the woman, he sets to work. As he scrapes the neatly cut pieces into the plastic bag, they are still writhing.

When I return to the house, Rhein is above in his studio. I listen at the foot of the stairs. Unable to hear the scrape of his palette knife, I am unsure whether to be pleased by the silence. Sometimes it can mean he is working: but sometimes it means that he is staring out at the lake. When he has spent hours like this, he will always come down in a black mood, but he will never tell me why. Still, it is better than the noise, for when his painting is going badly, he breaks things and his furious pacing rams the kitchen ceiling, sending flakes of whitewash fluttering to the tiled floor.

For no reason I can fathom, except perhaps the drive home past flower-fields stretching like rainbows to the horizon, I am hopeful. In the garden, the crocuses are burgeoning. I want to take some, set their pale insistence in an eggcup on the table. But if I do, he will frown at my frivolity. "You have butchered them," he will say, as he once said when I cut some daffodils. That is something about him I have grown used to: he will always repeat words without a single deviation from the way he strung them together the first time. Knowing this, I am never inclined to make the same mistake twice. But tonight there will be new words: a new frame of reference. Despite my hopefulness, I am afraid.

He has come down, his presence filling the air so that the walls seemed to shrink, close in tightly. By the time he had come, the sun had already deserted this old high-ceilinged kitchen. The snap of the light switch was not enough to dispel the shadows. I told him then, the words tumbling in a torrent as I served the food. He said nothing. He sat and ate. I could not bear it.

"What d'you think?" I pushed my plate of food aside. "I think nothing." He swirled the wine in his glass, his eyes watchful under hooded lids, a cat in a cage waiting for a child to stretch its hand between the bars.

I waited. It was only when his English slipped a little that I could decipher it. But still he did not speak.

"You must think something. It's a child."

His hand slammed the table and the glass spun, wine spilling blood across the light oak.

"It is a thing. A parasite. Feeding on you. I will tell you something." He turned to look at me, the words erupting from the hard rim of his mouth. "It will not feed on me."

I was frozen with it. For a long time there was silence.

The drip from the tap began to pound on the cracked enamel.

"You have heard me, yes?"

I nodded.

"When you get rid of it, I will have a vasectomy. This stupidity will not happen again."

"Stupidity. That's all it is to you."

"It was stupid to become impregnated."

"You make me sound like a cow. Like you had nothing to do with it."

"You were supposed to control it."

"For god's sake, Rhein, I couldn't take the pills. That time when I was sick" —

"You should have taken them."

"I couldn't. Doctor Bon made me stop while he gave me the

injections. And you ... you still wanted ..." I was bitter, remembering.

"You should have told me."

"I forgot. I forgot. How can you expect me to remember things like that when I'm sick."

He leaned forward. "That is not important now. When do you get rid of it?"

"I ... I didn't arrange anything." I gulped some wine.

"No!" The word thudded in my ear. He stood abruptly, his chair overturning to crack on the tiles.

"If that is what you want, you must leave. I made it clear to you from the first. I want no children. You agreed." He began pacing, his shadow hurled against the walls.

"I want to have it." I didn't think he heard above the staccato of his steps. But he stopped suddenly.

"Then go."

"Where? Where can I go? I've no money, nothing. Please." I turned to him. "Don't make me ..."

"It is your choice. I wash my hands. I will give you some money. You can go back."

I stood, screaming. "You know I can't go back, you know it. Don't say that to me."

"Then stay. Get rid of it." He jerked a bottle from the rack and began to open it, swearing as the cork split.

I was shaking. Once before he had been that cruel. He had gone to Ireland, tried to force me to go with him. But I could not go back. I had waited a long time for him to return, but when he did, he would not speak for the first ten days, he was in such a black sulk. Then he said, "It is primitive, your country, full of bleak landscapes. Never have I seen so many tones of grey. I painted much." He talked of when the crates of his paintings might arrive and when I had begun to relax, he said it.

"The house of your father is beautiful. Not at all the gothic horror you described." His words chilled me.

"What did you do?"

He shrugged, but his eyes were alert. "It seemed a pity to pass it. I was interested in its architecture, those Ionic columns."

"Liar."

He ignored me. "I called one day. Your father was kind enough to let me sketch it."

"Liar. You're lying."

"I will show you the sketch when it arrives. You will see it has been done from inside the grounds."

"I don't want to see it. You bastard. How dare you! I told you to stay away."

"Have you no wish to know how your parents are? What we talked of?"

"Fuck you! Fuck you for doing this!" I had run and locked myself in the cellar. Hours later I came out. But only when he had promised me that he'd said nothing to my parents about me, about where I was, and that he would never speak of it, never taunt me with it again.

Now, as he handed me a glass of wine, he repeated it, "Get rid of it."

The words began to pound inside my head keeping time with the tap. I drained the glass, the lightness filling me with courage. "I want to stay. And I want to have it. You'll feel different about ... Once it's born ..." I hiccuped, my voice caving, losing its conviction.

"Listen to me." He sat close, gripping my shoulders. "I do not want it, you understand?"

"But why? For god's sake tell me ..."

"This world is a sick place. I will not subject anyone else to it. Nor will I be tied to it any more than I can help."

"Then you might as well be dead."

"Precisely. That is what I strive for. To be dead alive. To feel nothing."

"What about me?"

"I want you. I have told you. But I will have no excess baggage."

"Sometimes we've been happy."

He laughed, the sound beating against my face.

"We are a lie. For those who face reality, there is no happiness. Look to you. You have run away from what you could not face. You hide here with me, ja?"

"And you? What great truths do you face? You're hiding too." I winced as his grip tightened.

"You stupid bitch. Listen to me. I hide from nothing. Nothing, you understand?" Jumping up, he released me and I shrank as he raised his hand. When the blow didn't come, I opened my eyes. He was standing at the window, staring through the blackness towards the lake.

I watched the rigid line of his back, his broad hands gripping the edge of the sink as though he would wrench it apart. "This time only, I will speak of it. Then again, never. You will not interrupt me. When I have finished, you will not interrogate me."

I stared at him. I never knew what to expect. Everything came in spurts from him, his anger, his need of me, his sudden obsessions with work. Even in his hair there was nothing uniform, no blending of colours. Instead, streaks of white slashed the black as effectively as paint.

"Now, listen to it," he rasped.

"My home was Bruckhausen, a small village on the East German border. The war was almost over. We were old men, children and the women. The young men were away fighting. All the German forces east of Danzig, isolated. The Russians were in Poland. We lived on rumours of the continuing advance of General Zhukov's armoured columns. One day word came that they had been sighted crossing the Brandenburg frontier. The next we heard that one of Zhukov's spearheads had reached the lower Oder near Kustrin.

We were all of us, trapped.

We ran to the church. The children were bundled to a corner. The adults talked. Later, my grandmother told me how it was decided. The thaw had already set in on the Oder, and the next morning at first light the people would go together to the river: to drown. The strongest among us would help those weak, hold the children under." He swung around suddenly and glared. Had I spoken? I didn't know. "You must understand what it was for us. These Russians, we had killed three millions of them, ja? They hated us deeply the same as we hated the Jews."

Striding to the table, he poured some wine. The bottle knocked erratically against the glass. And his eyes. Black with it. I didn't want to hear any more. But I was afraid to move. While he drank, I filled my own glass.

"I had twelve years then. Tall for my age. Greater than my grandmother." He paused, his raucous tone filling the room. "Oma made me promise when we got to the river, I would hold her under." He turned abruptly and flung his glass at the window. "I kept it!" The words were a hoarse roar above the shattering glass. When I opened my eyes his face was bleeding from several cuts. I tried to get up, but it was as if I had no legs. "You've cut ..."

"Shut up. Listen." His face contorted. He wiped a small dribble of blood that hovered on his eyebrow, streaking it across his forehead.

"When we reached the river, the Russians were already there, flanking the east bank. There were two divisions, the first on horseback. Behind them the heavy Stalin tanks of the infantry. Already people had begun jumping into the river. There was much screaming as the Russians drove their horses into the water. The current was swift with the pull of the Baltic thirty kilometres north. Some were swept downstream before the Russians could reach them. Others struggled with the soldiers and were stunned in the thrashing hooves of the horses. Many were drowned.

Oma never struggled. Not even when ... When I was sure it was done, I plunged into the mainstream, for swimming with the current. Suddenly I was seized on the collar, being pulled towards the east bank. I could not get at the rider. Even I kicked at his horse. It made no difference. That Russian bastard saved me." He ground glass underfoot. A cold wind ruffled his hair, carrying the strong briny tang of the lake into the room. Beyond the broken window, the clouds glowed with the faint rumour of moonlight.

"On the bank, there were many others that the Russians had pulled out."

"What happened?"

"Nothing! Nothing happened! All. All of it." The words snapped in the air. "For nothing. The Russians never harmed one of us. They had only seventy kilometres from Berlin. They were too busy on getting there, too busy to kill us. They continued to advance southwest, leaving a small garrison in the village."

"It wasn't your fault." I was sorry as soon as I'd spoken. He hated sympathy.

"You are stupid. There is no blame to apportion. Except, perhaps the superstitions, the fears, of the old. And my mother. The sow who bore me. She and several of the younger women hid in the church. Afraid to come to the river. Several days later, the bodies floated, some of them trapped in the thick bushes far down the bank: others snagged in the rocks of ice that had not yet thawed, their faces and bodies half eaten away. Oma was not among them." He came to the table, splashing more wine into his glass.

"By now, my mother was whoring with a Russian officer. I ran away. Our soldiers had launched a counter-defensive against the Russians on the Neisse. After three weeks of sneaking and crawling through the countryside, I managed to join them. They laughed at how crazy I was to fight. Nevertheless, they gave me a gun. But within weeks, the Russians burst from their bridgeheads across the river. We were defeated. Many of us were captured. I was ten years in one of their concentration camps."

I stared at him as he crossed to the wine rack, splinters of glass snapping on the tiles. I thought of those people he painted, their faces like cold, dead fish, my own among them. I saw then all it could ever be was this, cold and dead inside me, floating in its amniotic brine. I had no courage for it to be otherwise.

"Salut!" he said harshly and raised the bottle, drinking half its contents before he lowered it. I dragged myself from the chair and began to push the brush about the floor.

"Leave it. Come upstairs."

"You didn't have to break it. You didn't have to. You didn't." I heard the glass rattling and scraping under the brush, but I couldn't see it, everything was blurred. I knew then I was crying but I couldn't feel it, I could only feel what he'd done. "It was necessary. You wanted me to tell you. Now you must decide."

But it was already done. He had seen to that. "It's a mess. All a mess."

"Come." He took the brush from me.

"It will be a mess. A terrible terrible mess. Half-fleshed, like your bodies. And bones?" I looked up at him as he led me toward the door. "Will there be bones?"

"How many weeks' gestation have you?"

I wrenched myself from him, screaming. "I am not an animal. It is not an animal."

"That is precisely what it is, what we are. What other animal treats its own kind as ...? We are not even animals. We are savages."

"Fuck you. Just leave me alone."

"Very well. Nevertheless, you must remember. If you give that thing a life it will become an oppressor or victim. A wonderful choice for it, ja?" He strode to the door.

"What about me?"

"What of you?" He turned. "You will be the sow who bore it." The door crashed behind.

I sit at the table, my head laid on the wood. "Too busy to kill." And Rhein? Too full of it to live. I stay for a long while, hating him, picturing how it will be. Pieces of eel writhing in a sac: scraped away like his knife across the wooden palette. Every day he paints I will listen for it, just as every day he watches the lake.

It is still dark. Yet through the window comes the first stirring of the waterfowl, the widgeons, teal and mallard that nest in the sedge along the banks. Though it is not yet winter, I remember the goosander he once freed from the ice, carrying it into the house, his face grim, his hands torn from the saw-toothed edges of its bill. He was a long time fitting the splint on its forewing; the sleek feathers an irridescent quiver under his touch; the bird's frantic whistles piercing the walls of this room.

Later, nearer summer, we stood watching its awkward run to take wing from the garden. And his face. Losing some of its austerity.

The icy coldness drives me upstairs. He is awake, waiting in the dark, the window bare.

"I'll call Doctor Bon in the morning." I am shivering. "Optimal," he says, rubbing my back. But the cold is inside me.

"No more raw herring."

"Whatever." He rubs my skin more vigorously as we lie staring among the phosphorescent shadows the moonlit water casts about the walls of the room.

Mary E O'Donnell

Triptych
(From paintings by Markey Robinson)

1. Forgotten Dreams

But no dream is forgotten,
despite the wounded hunch of that woman's shoulders,
her dark weary shawl and the nameless presence
that bows her head.

           No dream is forgotten.
The cottages flash their wildness
in a glare of white walls, only the thatched roofs
sag a little. And the murked cloud
that presses into the mountain's thighs,
and the stark, brown tree,
will answer nothing for that woman
with her wounded hunch of shoulder.

I want to reach inside,
touch her, tell her that because she has
not forgotten, all is well.
Woman of the weary shawl and green skirt,
ecstatic mountain, close cottage, naked tree,
you who dream together a murmur of dark wounds —
           — no dream is ever forgotten.

2. The Soft Earth

Elemental triad of earth, air, water:
the road can only lead to the sky,
and that textured paleness only to water,
where forked sails breast the breeze
                                    like swallows.
Earth, air, water, a self-adoring beast,
lithe limbs of a presence
to quicken the heart,
                          that could break it ...

3. The Quiet Hours

The child's thumb has warts.
I feel them when we two stroll at our ease
to the water's edge, beyond the glaring walls
of houses, down the sandy path,
our feet seeing the stray boulders
coughed up by angry mer-men.
We say little, beyond wondering
if a great ship might pass.
Her eyes follow a quiet brown sail
as it cuts across a dream.
Our thoughts, our chance words
belong to the ocean, drift towards the deep,
full of turquoise ease,
trawling us
            from the sureties of dry land

Old Gardens Are Not Relevant
(A Hungarian woman remembers the late forties)

1.

She was brought to church in summer,
slept in my arms as July
stifled our breath.
We passed perfumed gardens,
ladies, men who stood quietly.
Maids in starched frills
worked like strange butterflies,
while the fields were waving.
There were storks on the smokestacks,
a good sign, they said,
It was a quick baptism,
beneath a blue and yellow cupola.
But she never knew a day's health,
and people asked what birth-devil
sat on her cradle,
what demon regarded my sleep
in the months before.

2.

When she was six,
I brought her again
on the sourest day of the year,
the cupola above in a sheath of frost.
He poured water again,
wished good health on her head,
called the potentest graces
to enter her.
On the way home we stopped,
took tea and cakes in a yellow café.
Again there were ladies,
maids in starched frills.
Outside, a beggar avoided the sleet.
We watched as we ate.
Since then she's never looked back,
strong and wilful as a mother could wish.

3.

I pity women with sickly children.
The smokestacks were crushed,
old gardens are not relevant.
Today, they'd wait a long time
for a second, saving ritual
beneath the infinite lights
of a blue and yellow cupola.

Reading The Sunflowers in September

These days she walks to the sunflowers.
You never know whether she'll make it,
her bones having grown in recent times.
Such starvation is an art:
Admire her craft as she upbraids
a summer gluttony, tears sheets from herself,
inspired by shrinkage.

She reads sunflowers daily,
the spindles of her fingers reach out,
stroke yellow ellipses
as if each petal were a sign.
What really holds her are the seeds,
tucked tight like critical reviews
within a yellow convention.
They swell and separate while autumn
seems to idle, enchant her hunger
all the more, telling tales, gaze
like a thousand eyes at the sun's path.

She is bent on hers,
knows what she creates will have it all —
the Word made genderless.
These days she walks to the sunflowers.
When the seeds drop,
when petals shrink to skeletal,
she'll have made it.

Maeve Binchy

A Minute Late

The first time she went to America she heard the expression.
They used it about the uncle who was a bit slow.

"Oh Harry, he's a fine guy, always a minute late but the salt of
the earth is Harry."

Jess had thought they meant he was unpunctual.

"Doesn't he have a watch?" she had asked innocently. In this
land of plenty where there were three bathrooms in a family
home, where there was a clock on every wall, surely their Uncle
Harry would have had his own timepiece.

They had laughed at the eighteen year old Jess affectionately
as people seemed to have laughed gently all their lives.

She didn't feel that they were laughing *at* her, no she wasn't
paranoid, she told herself firmly, but people developed a sort of
indulgence towards her that sometimes she found very hard to
take.It was only the expression for heaven's sake, a minute late
... how could anyone be expected to know what it meant,
coming from a different culture? And she got it very quickly,
what they meant was that Harry wasn't the full shilling. Now
there was an expression, Jess thought triumphantly. Face a smart
snappy Yank with a phrase like that and see what he made of it.

But oddly that expression stayed around the edges of her
mind and irritated her. It seemed like some kind of reproach.
There were people who had inner clocks and were always alert
and understanding and there were those who were a minute
late. Never literally but in getting the point, in seeing the
advantage, in taking up the trend.

Jess was punctual to the point of obsession, she was always
standing twenty minutes early on the corner where she had
arranged to meet a friend. But she had the feeling that she might
in fact be someone that the world considered slightly slow. And
it irritated her more than she could say.

Because it was so unfair. At school Jess had been called
Jacinta, a great many girls were. There had been a great
devotion to the children of Fatima and the name was as
common as Mary for a while. Her little sister Fiona couldn't
manage the whole word so it had become Jess. It was nicer, Jess
thought, and in a more secular world too it was easier to

explain. People thought it was short for Jessica. It was like a name out of a book. She had been bright at school. She remembered the nuns reading Jacinta Murphy's essay out to the class more than once. She was always in an Honours class. She had been a prefect and second Head. When Dolores who was the real Head Girl got jaundice the Easter before the Leaving Jess had been Acting Head. She had made a speech of thanks to a TD, she had done the presentation to a retiring Reverend Mother. Her school reports had used words like Bright, and Has Mastered This Subject ... and even Excellent. Nowhere had they said she was plodding, diligent or doing her best. And her Leaving Certificate results were good too. Four Honours. Four passes. Back in 1956 that was very very good. That was long before Points and Groups and the terrible competition of today's world.

But it was the world Jess lived in and she went to University College Dublin, as her brother Feargal had before her and as Fiona would do after. In the strange first year with its swirling masses of people Jess could never have been thought backward. No, there was no way she didn't join everything that there was to be joined. Her family lived five miles away from Stephen's Green so she cycled in each day. There were lots of friends from school to start with, Dolores was there, and three other girls from her class. It was never lonely for Jess as it was sometimes for the girls who came up from the country, who didn't know people and who went to hostels or to a digs. And in the holidays she did what other girls did. She went to Spain to learn Spanish and mind horrifically spoiled Spanish children the year she was seventeen, and the year she was eighteen she went to see her American cousins. When she was nineteen she went to work in London for the long hot summer of 1959 and then she got her degree. A perfectly respectable Two Two. That meant a Second Class Honours Degree. Grade two, she remembered telling her grandmother, in case Gran didn't know the terminology. Gran *did* know and told her so forcibly.

"Don't mind Jess," they said. "She likes everything explained nice and neatly, she was always the same, even with her doll's house. Everything had to be laid out just so, and she'd say this is the kitchen, this is the bedroom ..."

Her mother and father had laughed, and grown-up Feargal, now a qualified engineer laughed, and Fiona about to set out herself for University laughed.

Jess felt a dull ache of anger inside her. Everyone seemed to be smiling at her and speaking as if she were still laying out a doll's house. She was twenty years of age, she was a graduate for god's sake. Why were they so unbearably patronising?

But it was her graduation day, and here they all were at an expensive hotel for lunch. It would be ludicrous to pick some kind of fight. Jess smiled hard to beat back the tears pricking in her eyes. And as she smiled she caught sight of herself in a mirror behind where Mother and Gran were sitting. She looked like a grinning idiot. She looked as if she wasn't all there. Perhaps this was why they spoke to her so gently and still talked in terms of doll's houses and playpens. Perhaps in their eyes Jess hadn't moved very much further ahead.

That night she went to the graduation ball with a heavy heart. She had gone in a party of twelve, they had all paid for their own tickets, boys and girls who were not doing lines, not in love but who felt a great solidarity, perched as they were on the edge of a new life. Jess danced mainly with Brian who had fancied her a year ago.

"You look very well considering" he said, as they twirled around the room.

"Considering what?" Jess had been in a heavy mood all afternoon. She felt very little excitement as she dressed for the dance with Fiona sitting and watching without comment. She felt the red dress had been a mistake, it drained a lot of the colour away from her face. She thought she looked wan and foolish as she peered at the crowded mirror in the Ladies' room.

"Considering you must be clinically insane. You cover it up I'll grant you, but I'd say most of the brain cells are gone."

He was totally unprepared for her reaction.

White as a sheet she dropped her arms from his shoulders and looked at him open mouthed and stricken.

"Jess ... Jess, for god's sake, what is it ...?"

Around them people laughed and bumped into them.

"What you said ..."

"It was a joke," Brian looked worried now. "Jesus, god, Jess, it was a joke. JOKE. You must have heard of them."

"Why did you say I must be insane ...?"

"Because you didn't come away with me that weekend ... last year. Because you never come off with me ... I was just saying you're mad to pass up a lovely body like mine. Mind too." Brian looked bewildered. To his great relief some colour seemed to be returning to Jess at last.

He led her back to their table and poured her a glass of orange from the big glass jug on the table and a dart of gin from the quarter bottle in his pocket. He looked around furtively lest a waiter see how the steep hotel prices for liquor were being avoided.

"If I had gone to bed with you, would that have been more normal?"

"It would certainly have been very nice, still would. Will perhaps?"

Brian looked optimistic.

"No, I mean is that what other people do? People like Dolores and Judy and everyone ...?" Her face was eager, she was determined to know.

"Well, lord, Jess, even if I knew ... I wouldn't tell you ... I mean people don't tell that sort of thing do they ...?"

"No, they don't," Jess shook her head sadly.

"But it's more and more common certainly" Brian said, anxious not to lose the high ground.

"I didn't realise ..." Jess was thoughtful. "And how is it nobody gets pregnant or anything?"

"Well I understand they take precautions."

"But we can't buy precautions here, they don't sell them" Jess was confused.

"Day trips to Belfast. Thursdays" said Brian. "I hear," he added lamely.

"And that all works. Nothing else?" Jess sounded factual as if she were asking the times a cinema performance began. It was somewhat disconcerting.

"Yes, well, I think probably they take a bit of timing into account as well."

"Timing?"

Brian was looking increasingly ill at ease.

"Let's go on dancing, that's a Bill Hayley" he said.

"You asked me last year to go to bed with you about twelve times. Now that I'm agreeing you say there's a Bill Hayley number ..."

"You're agreeing?" Brian's face lit up. "I thought you were just debating a point or analysing something, you know the way you do."

"No, I don't. What's the way I analyse things ...?"

"Oh go on Jess, you know. The way you are, pausing, thinking, deliberating, and then nodding in agreement once you've understood."

"I've always understood" she said, tears starting in her eyes.

"Well, you just said this minute that you didn't realise people went to bed together." He was stung by the unfairness.

"I said I didn't know *our* kind of people did, and I was filling myself in. What do you mean timing, do you mean like the safe period?"

Brian looked left and right.

"Yes, in a manner of speaking."

"And which *is* the safe time? No, stop looking at me like that. I never needed to know before so I didn't bother crowding my mind with it. Now I do need to know. It might be safe for me tonight."

Brian leaned towards her and kissed her on the nose. "I don't think these things should be done in such a hurry," he said tenderly. Jess felt the familiar wave of impatience. He was talking like everyone talked to her sooner or later.

"Have you gone off me? Is that it?"

"I'll always be fond of you, dear Jess" he said. "And now that he's changed to Buddy Holly will you dance with me?"

"I guess it doesn't matter any more" Jess said. That was the title of the song. "It's prophetic in a way. It *doesn't* matter any more.'"What? Sleeping with people?" Brian was alarmed.

"No. I mean everything. It doesn't matter. No one's ever going to understand." She sounded resigned.

"You're too aware, you worry too much about how you react to the world and how it reacts to you. Honestly, that's all" he was reassuring.

"No, it's the reverse, I haven't worried enough. But I'll start tomorrow."

Brian watched her uneasily as she danced, her eyes too bright, her laugh too forced. He watched as she danced with Denis, close smoochy dancing. Denis who'd get up on anyone. He watched with saddened eyes as she left the ballroom draped around Denis.And they never came back to the flat where everyone else was having more drink, sausages and a sing song.

By new year's day 1960, Jess had completed her intensive secretarial course. Her friends had either stayed on at University to study for an MA or do one of the short diploma courses leading to teaching or being a librarian.

Sometimes she heard her mother's friends asking was there any sign of Jess losing her heart. Her mother always sighed and said thank god not a sign that was ever known. And even from the kitchen or the hall Jess could feel them smiling kindly about her.

Sometimes she heard people say that it was odd of her to have spent all those years at University and then got a job that she might have been able to go to straight from school. But her father always said that a University education was never wasted and he was glad to have been able to give that to Jess. She didn't know if he actually ever said it or if she just read it into his tone but she definitely thought that he said "She'll always have that even if she has nothing else".

Jess was invaluable in the office, she knew where everything was and how everything was done. Mr Power asked her to call him Jonathan. After five years she decided to get a small flat of her own.

Her parents were startled.

"Will you be able to manage?" her mother asked.

"I think I can make breakfast and take my things to the launderette all right" Jess said.

"But why leave a nice comfortable home for no reason?" her father asked.

"Fiona's in a flat" Jess said, "She's not married. Feargal's in a flat. He's not married. You play a lot of Bridge in the evenings. You won't be lonely or anything."

"I suppose it's all for the best really," her father said anxiously to her mother. They spoke as if she weren't there. She distinctly remembered a conversation like that when she was five and they were deciding to let her out on the footpath with her tricycle in their quiet road. Nothing had changed. Nothing ever would.

She was very surprised when Jonathan Power asked her to dinner. "Will I bring my pad?" she asked.

He roared laughing.

"No, seriously?" she persisted.

"I'm asking you to dinner because you are a lovely, charming companion. You must know that. Surely you know that, Jess?"

"I'm a bit slow" she said.

"It's part of your charm," he said. And she knew that it was part of her as her soul was. She had tried to be so bright and so quick and so ahead of the game in that office. And now the truth was actually stated and defined. She was slow Jess Murphy. Slow. But charming. Her slowness was part of her charm. How great. How lovely at a quarter of a century to know that this was the diagnosis. He held her hand during the second evening out, he asked her to meet his mother after their fifth outing. A month later he asked if he could be invited to her home.

"Whatever for?" Jess asked, interested. "You don't play Bridge."

"No but I'd like to meet your parents. To let them get to know me."

"Why Jonathan?"

He kissed her lips. "Don't ever change. Promise me" he begged.

She went over that sentence. Even after he had asked her to marry him and she had said yes, Jess kept thinking "Stay as slow as you are, don't let a thing ever change you." It sounded like a funeral march.

Her parents said she was a dark horse. Imagine all this going on under their noses.

"I didn't know it was going on. Truthfully" Jess said, and they looked at each other worried, and believing her utterly.

On their honeymoon they met a group of Irish people in Torremolinos, the chat was fast and funny. Jess sat there and listened as they talked about the Bank Strike and Dev going for a second term as President, they all seemed to know everything that was happening in the World Cup and had views on Mary Quant getting an OBE and the film star Ronald Reagan becoming Governor in California.

"I'm sorry I know so little. I can't think how I missed knowing all these things" she said.

"It's the way you are, thoughtful" Jonathan said.

"That can't be right, otherwise I'd be full of thoughts."

"No, no, no" he soothed. "Look at how well you adapt to things. Like making love for example. I bet you thought you'd never take to that like you do."

Jess was silent. She remembered what Brian had told her long, long ago about her wanting to analyse and define everything. She hadn't found it necessary to tell Jonathan about Denis. Which had not been anything to write home about. As if you would ever write home about anything like that. These phrases were very odd. More and more she found her head filling up with them. Proverbs, clichés, old sayings. And if you tried to think about them, a lot of them were meaningless.

She had three children in three years, and then they thought that was enough, and of course by 1969 there were better ways of making sure that you didn't conceive than by hasty day trips on Thursday to Belfast.

There was the visit to the doctor and the prescription for a pill to cope with menstrual irregularity.

There was a wonderful woman who came when the first child was born. She was called a mother's help, but really she was a housekeeper. She did everything for the family. She was a deserted wife, she told Jess, she did not intend to marry again, she had no children of her own, so she was no trouble to them. Others envied Jess for having Pat. One day Jess overheard her younger sister Fiona saying that of course Pat would stay for ever in that household and why not? Poor Jess was far too thick to see that her own role had been completely taken over, Pat didn't have to deal with another woman's normal wish to be mistress in her own house. Jess thought about it for a long time. But couldn't see how it was true. Here she was in 1979, aged 39 with three children all going to school, with a part-time job in her husband's office where she was greatly respected, not only because she was the wife of Mr Power but because she literally did know where everything was and how everything was done. She didn't have to scrub floors and stand in queues in supermarkets or hang clothes out on lines. She had time for her children. Fiona, who was a high flier in her job, had no time for her two and her husband was widely rumoured to be having an affair. So what was so dim and thick about Jess, Jess wondered to herself often.

They had their twenty year reunion as they had always planned they would do. Dolores was now the leading Women's Rights campaigner in the country, Judy one of Dublin's best known Society Hostesses. Denis had been dried out and was very anxious to put almost everyone else in the universe off drink as well. Brian was a teacher but was known all over the country as well as in England and America as a poet. He had brought his most recent collection as a gift to Jess.

"Look, there's one dedicated to me!" she cried, pleased.

"Yes. Read it another time" he said. He looked at her with a half smile. She still looked soft and innocent, her flyaway fair hair and her clear untroubled, pale blue eyes.

"I'll read it now" Jess said.

She sat in a corner and read it over and over. It was impossible to understand because it was all set in a farmyard, and the chickens were coming up to the trough to eat the meal, one chicken kept getting squeezed out, it was behind the others. Meal after meal it was unable to get to the feeding place. It never seemed too concerned. It pecked around for grubs on the earth around the farmyard.

But the farmer's wife saw it and saved special things for that small bird. So that in the end it managed to thrive more than all the others. It had lost nothing by not getting there in time. The farmer's wife had capital letters. Jess read it three times. "It's lovely," she said politely.

"It has won prizes. I'd never have written it without you." Brian said.

Jess looked at him, pleased. It was nice to have been loved by him all those years ago. He must have loved her really if he thought of picking one of the poems to dedicate to her.

"Did you see yourself that this is what happened? That there was a Farmer's Wife who cared?" he asked.

"I see you have that with capitals. Why is that?"

"I suppose it's god really. God or fate or whatever you like to call it" he said.

"Like, it's god who looks after chickens and sees they don't get left out?" Her eyes took on that strained look they did when she was trying hard to understand.

She was annoyed that he was looking at her so pityingly.

After all, *he* was the one who had been in love with *her* and carried a torch for her for nearly two decades. Why else would he have gone through his collection of poems and found one to dedicate to her? Jess wished in a way that he had put her name on a better one. A more grown up one than this kind of fairy tale about farmers' wives and chickens.

Still, it was good to have your name in a poetry book. She would show it to the children tomorrow. Already twelve, eleven and ten they were showing alarming signs of talking down to her.

As if she didn't understand things as quickly as everyone else.

Eithne Strong

September Song

One of these days I'll take myself in hand, get
some money together and buy a small car that works.
I'm fed-up with the discouraging old carcass
crouched by the pavement, its every joint
and muscle geared to misbehave or block —
a surly clogged-up lump, intractable. It is
too like myself. I need a car that will encourage me
that will, for instance, keep the rear-view mirror
steady and operate with soothing reflex
as do the cars of friends who give me
lifts. I'd like a realistic backward measure:
I tend to put a lot down to the stiffness in my neck.

I'll get my eyes seen to before that.
There are things they can do these days:
there's that laser operation —
gives you the shivers when you think of it
although I know a teenager who swears
by it. Her father had money and didn't shun
the price. She said securely,
"My Daddy loves me." I have
no Dad and spare money never a bit
but I'll get it together somehow for he's costly,
this tricky eye-man, a defected Slav —
I tend to put a lot down to poor sight.

And in my new car that works
giving me a true rear view
maybe I could venture alone this time to Cahirciveen,
attempt long slow ways to Vienna or Aix-
en-Provence, along boreens — they don't know
that word in Europe — for, even
with my new laser view forward
and my steady rear-view mirror, I'll still
need boosting, will wish to keep clear
of all carrier trucks that brute the ground,
ten-wheel furies to suck you in their violent pull
and, like some memories, blast a courage mostly fear.

An Féar Nach Stopfaidh

I mbliana tá lámh in uachtar
　　ag an bhféar orm;
níor mhaolaigh ar a fhás
　　ó mhí Márta,
mé ag ól mo chuid allais
　　ag stracadh
leis an meaisín bacach bainte.

Bhíos ag ceapadh go bhfaighinn sos
　　um Iúil — babhta seisce
b'fhéidir, ach ní raibh lá gan bháisteach
　　ag brostú an fhásra,
is arís, maidir le Lúnasa, bhí sin
　　ar an Lúnasa
ba fhliche i stair an chéid.

Teacht an Fhómhair, adúrt, beidh tuirse
　　ar an bhféar, rachaidh a chodladh,
ligfidh scíth. Ach beag baol air:
　　Meán Fómhair, Deireadh Fómhair —
ba iad na míonna ba ghrianmhaire fós linn,
　　corr-chioth leo nár lean
ach a dheol an glasra le goile.

Inniu Lá Samhna, boige san aer;
　　osclaím na dóirse, líonann
grian an pasáiste a bhí gruama anois beag,
　　lasmuigh éalaíonn an fómhar: duilleoga
ina sciatháin ar foluain nó go socraíonn
　　go réidh órga ar an bhféar
atá glas, bíogach mar an earrach.

The Year Of The Grass

This year the grass got/the better of me;/it has not stopped growing/.since March/and I've been sweating like/a pig, struggling/with my bockety lawnmower.

I was thinking I might get a break/around July — a dry spell,/possibly, but each day rain came/bringing on the growth,/and then again as to August,/that was/the wettest August of the century.

Come Autumn, I thought, the grass/will be tired, it will rest,/go to sleep. But not a bit of it:/September, October —/they were the sunniest months yet,/just the odd shower which/the grass sucked down, then sprang.

Today, November Day, the air is soft;/I open doors, sunshine amazes/the passage sullen a moment since;/outside Autumn steals about:/leaves, as wings, float, to settle gently/their yellow on the grass/which is vivid, thrusting like the spring.

(Trans. Eithne Strong)

Yellow Joke

I have a great liking
for the ridiculous,
the way it makes
a fatal hole in solemnity,
letting in
the light of laughter.

The sky cracked
and there was a huge laughing.

Lightning ridicules, splitting
pompous clouds, rending
their bloated threat
to the splendid mockery
of thunder,
the elemental hilarity
of crazy rain.

Let us enjoy the banana skin
bringing dictators to the ground.

Linda Anderson

Blinding

1 Lucy

I put out my eyes. Because I must be invisible. Out of your sight.
Now you dare not see me. I am what you cannot countenance.
Rape of the head. Bulges around the weeping slits. The slimy
severed stalks of my eyes.
I am a honeycomb of holes. A holey woman. Pores, sense
organs, orifices. The gape between the legs. The cavity of the
womb. Multitude of entrances. Entrancements. Honeycomb.
There is a man who loves me. He compared me to milk and
honey. He steals milk from the goats, plunders honey from the
bees. He thought I was a flow of nurture and sweetness.
I am fire and gall. He called my hair a redgold flame and said
my eyes burned as if from caverns. But he imagined a tame
fireside, not a blazing forest.
He loves me so much, my devoted suitor! He loves me to death.
"I have eyes only for you." he said, blocking out the sun. Love!
He is an old man, lonely and afraid. He wants to hide from
death by draping my flesh over his.
I refused to marry. I would not lie impaled beneath him,
inhaling his dirty breath. I did not want to wake up with him
thick upon me. I would not bear a flock of children. Tiny hands
to scatter me. I am I. Sole. One. Unwon.
I was happy before his glance felled me. When I was a child I
visited the shrine of Saint Bridget and I heard her speak to me.
She whispered: "Lucy, you will be a light unto the world!"
A light unto the world! Not one old man's delight!
O little, little man! Love made him spiteful. He denounced me to
the persecuting authority. The judge ordered me to be violated
in a brothel. Tortured. Hot lead poured into my ears. My breasts
slashed. Love broke me to bits. Cracked my I. Turned my aye
into Please No Please No Please No ...
I gutted my eyes. I wanted to tear out the tear ducts forever! I
sent the mess to my lover. Titbits on a dish. Two glistening
globes. Yes, feast your gaze on that! You will never be rid of my
terrible stare.
But why has no one ever seen *me*? I live in my body, not his

mind! Nor yours! Do not cast me as a saint. Some scrawny icon with neat wounds and no breasts. Don't invent a serene uplifted face. Don't add a golden nimbus nor any downpour of heavenly balm to cancel my pain. Forget miracles! No missing eye grows back.

And do not tell yourself that I was passionless! There was a man who could make me howl and claw the ground. I was true to him though we never met.

I lie here quietly on my bier. The fragrance of flowers penetrates my chamber although the door is sealed. i thought I would be free. That they would let me rot on this border between life and death. But my punishment is not over. The judge has ordered me to be burnt. "Better to marry than to burn" the churchmen say. Now I know what they mean.

2 Jocasta

Loving you was no crime, Oedipus! My lover, my son!
I gave you your body and then you gave me mine! Brought me alive again! I delivered you and then you delivered me! I smelled of your seed as you once smelled of my milk. Like animals, warm and reeking of each other. I did not know that you were my son restored to me. Wouldn't all mothers and sons fall in love if they were separated and reunited much later?
You are the man I made! Once you lay beneath my heart. Our blood mingled. I dreamed your face before you were born. Your coming burst me asunder. Astonished, unhealed, I held you. Your mouth clamped to one nipple made the other spurt with jealousy.
I tingled in all the places I had never been kissed.
I loved your drool and your golden dung. Shameless, yes! Then and now.
I am not peculiar. Every woman is an outlaw, guarding her secrets. Mumbling her riddles at your stony walls. A mother is supposed to be a milky mammal, an oozing sack of moisture. Reduced to pure matter. Mater. And yet she must be pure spirit as well, a white blur of solicitude! I will tell you what a mother is. A mass of sensation. A caterwaul of yearning! I revelled in you, my first love. Sin was to lie and lie in your father's rank bed. Stiff and cold as he pumped me and winced on top of me. He was overjoyed at first when he managed to sire you. But then the old fool listened to the oracle and began to be terrified of you. He looked at a babe-in-arms and saw an executioner ten feet tall. Tore you away from me. Pierced your feet with thongs. Left you maimed and exposed on a mountainside.
Oh, why do you fear me, Oedipus? Do you think I would put you back in my womb? Entomb you? It is your dead father who will bury you! Defy him, Oedipus! Defy all the grim old men who hate their sons. Why does war never disappear? Because old men need wars to devour their sons. The programme of extermination is never over. Always a new yield of youths, potent usurpers, to be cut down. Rebel against the vicious fathers, Oedipus, and the mean gods who drive their stakes into you. Punctured feet and now, lacerated eyes! Hideous re-enactment! You blinded yourself with my beautiful glittering brooch. For an innocent breach of the law, Oedipus. Your language has lost its senses. Kin does not equal sin. Do not be mute as well as blind. Do not bow your head. I loved you and I love you still. I have never been more pure. Do not satisfy your

father's hatred. Do not woo your mother's death. The future can always be rewritten, Oedipus.

3 Peter

I had a real job. Five thousand under me and no complaints.I was a gravedigger. Used to earn extra cash down the morgue, cleaning up the bad car crash cases. Mush and slime and caked blood. O Death, where is Thy stink? Everywhere.

Never look down on a gravedigger. Remember, he's the one shall look down on you! RIP, all you VIPs. Very important persons! I gave you special treatment. I loved you to bits. I could make you sit up in your coffins and play the ventriloquist with you. The best one I ever got was a lady magistrate! Gave her a good shaking. "You'll never sentence anyone again, Bitch!"

The other lads thought they were hard but I shocked them, I kicked death. Played footie with a skull more than once. Little Peter! My dad used to call me his "favourite daughter". Always hiding behind my mam's skirts, he said. Face half-buried in the folds. Afraid to go outside. Everybody laughed at me. Split their sides laughing at my stutter and my skinny legs. My dad gave up on me, he said. Because I couldn't talk right and couldn't even walk before I was near two and he bought me some reinforced boots.

After I was caught, my brother asked me why I did it. "I don't like prostitutes," I said. "Neither do I," he said.

My tools were a lump-hammer, a knife, and a screwdriver. Their skulls smashed like eggshells. I split their guts. I never fucked them, that's a lie. I arranged them. I wanted to show them for what they were.

There was the one I did on a piece of wasteground just outside the city. After applying the hammer, I pulled down her bra to bunch her tits. Then I crammed horsehair from an old sofa into her mouth. Tart became art. I was the Picasso of the rubbish dumps.

She rotted for a month before they discovered her. Oh, she horrified them!

I was in God's hands. No one believes me about that in Bingley. I was digging a grave. My feet were five feet below the surface. The earth was hard and I paused to rest. Suddenly I heard it, echoes, a kind of singing. I had to climb out of the grave to follow it. I mounted the hill. Right to the top, overlooking the valley.

Rain began to fall. I was so calm and happy. Jesus had spoken to me. I knew I was chosen for something.

My last one was a student, they say. Like my wife. I felt a bit sad about that. But why do they have to act like whores?

Even my mother turned out bad. My dad found her out. He played a trick on her. Rang up pretending to be her fancy-man and invited her to a hotel. When she arrived, we were all there to greet her: Dad, Maureen, Sonia and me! My dad upended her bag and out spilt a new frilly nightdress ...

A student. According to them. My thirteenth victim. Unlucky thirteen. She kept looking at me. Looking right at me with her brazen cruel eyes. I perforated them for her. Well, gentlemen prefer blinds, I told her.

The pupil of the eye is a hole. A hole to trap light. A nothing that expands and contracts. Like a womb. A void.

I stuck my pin into nothing.

4 Toshiko

6 August 1945. That was my deathday. I survived it. Subvived it. You know about that day, don't you? The river choked with bodies. The blinded people running, their skin fluid and dripping like candlewax. The black rain and charred birds that fell over the city. Light is a torture to me. I live blindfolded in a windowless and muffled room. No chink of light must enter. I am entombed and forgotten. An Egyptian mummy in my sealed and airless dark. But I can speak. I speak to you from my afterlife. Will you listen?

I have become antennae. The sores on my skin have grown ridged and purple. Like emergency eyes against the atrocious night. My body is a night-watchman. My small burial chamber echoes with cries. I hear the pleas of the raped child. The soldier's boot crashing through the door. I see the thatched villages burn. Somewhere in Africa a woman is stooping over a brown puddle. She hesitates a moment. Cups the water in her hands and drinks. I am the woman. I am the dirty water.

Prayer is listening. Listing. I count the sorrows.

I am *hibakusha*, an atomic leper. Banished from your sight. One of the scarred that you are scared to see. There are so many of us. We blur. We lack definition. We blaze in miniature behind a black shimmer of time and distance.

There are light bulb factories in Hiroshima now. Light out of darkness. Commerce rules ...

I watch and wait for the next Blinding. For our mind is set on slaughter. I don't know why. Perhaps you imagine some moment of illumination before the end? But the moth shrivelling in the flame sees nothing. Perhaps you imagine nothing and that is your trouble?

You must open your eyes or burn.

The bomb they dropped over Hiroshima was named "Thin Boy".

My name was Toshiko.

5

Hills in early morning light. Profusion of blackgreen trees.
Swirls of birds. A man with a gun.
A hawk glides into the killing field of vision. Alights on a
branch. The sniper raises his weapon. Now the barrel juts from
between his eyes like an iron proboscis. Already he feels a
voluptuous shiver of sorrow for the proud dead bird.
"No! No!"
A woman is running towards him. Shouting.
"YOU CANNOT KILL A HAWK!"
He falters. He is reduced to choice. The woman stops in her
tracks.
They stare at each other. Above them, sensed rather than seen, a
beating of wings. The wild bird soars. Untargeted. Free.

Biddy Jenkinson

Belvedere (An Grá Cuntraphointeach)

'Bhfuil 'fhios a't an liteagraf a rinne Escher
sa bhliain 1958, an Belvedere,
foirgneamh aerach Iodálach
a chuirfeadh le craobhacha thú
mar go bhfuil iomrall súl á chur ort
ach nach léir láithreach céard é
nó conas ...

Tá cúrsa amháin faoin urlár thuas
mar a fhéachann bean amach ort,
cúrsa eile faoin urlár thíos
mar a dtugann fear a chúl ort.

Níl dealramh leis
ach fós
dearbhaíonn na súile
go bhfuil na cúinní, na huillinneacha,
na hingir, na línte ar fad, fíor ...
gur áras ar fónamh é
an t-áras seo nach féidir.

De réir a chéile tagann an inchinn ar réiteach.
Tá gach mír ar leith fíor ann féin.
Is iad na ceangail atá cleasach ...
An colún sin a éiríonn ar chúl
ach a thugann taca don urlár thuas
ar an taobh is cóngaraí duit, abair ...

Léaspáin a cuireadh ar do shúile.
Is léir nach féidir an t-áras seo a shlánú
ach le draíodóireacht.

D'ainneoin sin, léimeann do shúile ó fhírinne go fírinne
ar na ceangail bhréige
mar gur deacair fírinní scaipthe, contráilte, a fhulaingt
gan sintéis a bhrú orthu.

Nach fíor, a chroí?
Nach fíor? Nach
fíor?

Belvédère (Amour en contrepoint)

Tu connais cette Lithographie d'Eschers,
Le Belvédère,1958;
 un édifice italien spacieux
à te rendre démente
car tes yeux sont abusés
ce n'est pourtant pas évident
où se trouve la duperie
ni comment cela fonctionne ...

L'étage en-haut, où une femme t'observe
s'en va d'un côté.
L'étage en-bas où un homme se détourne de toi
s'en va d'un autre.

C'est vraiment impossible
pourtant
l'oeil insiste
que les coins, angles,
perpendiculaires, toutes lignes, sont vrais
que cette maison impossible
est réelle.

Peu à peu l'esprit arrange les choses.
Chaque élément est vrai
ce sont les liaisons qui déçoivent
cette colonne qui s'élève à l'arrière pourtant
supporte l'étage supérieur, proche.

Tes yeux furent éblouis.
Ceci est un immeuble qui ne peut exister que par magie.

Néanmoins l'oeil saute
de vrai en vrai sur de faux rapports
car il est dur de supporter
des vérités contraires dispersées
sans leur forcer une synthèse.

N'est-il pas vrai, chérie?
N'est-il pas vrai?
N'est-il pas
vrai?

(Trans. Mireille Harnett).

Don chrann Ginko baineann a fhásann i gcarrchlós "Safeway" ar MacArthur Boulevard i Washington DC

Ní bhítear ag filíocht ort in aon chor anseo,
a Ghinko,
a chroí.
Ní bhítear.

Croitheann tú anuas torthaí mar chacanna beaga crua
a d'fháiscfí trí sceo since ar bhundún linbh
is ramhraíonn tú an carrchlós in aon bhleaist bhréan
go mbímid ag sliodarnach.

Dá mbainfeá siar beag as do nádúr, a chroí,
mura rachfá thar fóir ...
mura mbeifeá chomh scaoilte ...
Is cac thú ar eineach antaiseipteach ocastóirí.

Salaíonn tú bróga a leanann orthu isteach sa stóras
is do shliocht orthu
ag bréanadh an aeir
a cumhraíodh ar mhórchostas.

Sraoill tú a lig d'íochtar go talamh mar mhagadh
is bíonn ar dhaoine macánta siúl tharat
amhail is dá mbeidís ag siúl ar uibheacha
— is gan uathu, chuile sheans, ón siopa féin,
ach coiscíní, b'fhéidir.

Is a Ghinko, a chroí, táim leat
— cé nach ndéarfainn amach é

Bhí an toradh beag dóchasach a phiocas den talamh
is do bhiaiste á chartadh acu
cruinn,
fuar,
ionraic,
is luigh sé im dhearna go truamhéalach.
Leagas anuas go hómósach é ar dhíon *Porsche*
lena thabhairt i ngrinneas

Is ní raibh de rogha agam ina dhiaidh sin
ach mo phócaí a líonadh go tapa
lena raibh fágtha de d'uaillmhianta
is suí sa bhus id bhréantas
— mo luisní dearga ag briseadh suanaíocht an gheimhridh id
    shíolta —
gur bhaineamar áit oiriúnach amach cois abhann
mar ar chuireas thar do cheann iad
a Ghinko, a bhean.

A Ginko la femelle du parking "Safeway"
Boulevard McArthur, Washington DC

Ils ne te composent pas d'odes, ici
Ginko
Chérie
Ils n'en n'écrivent pas.

Tu ponds des fruits comme des petites selles dures
forcées à travers un film de zinc sur l'anus d'un enfant
Encombrant le parking d'une explosion puante
jusqu'à ce qu'on glisse.

Si tu pouvais au moins te restreindre un peu, ma chère,
si tu n'exagérais pas,
si tu n'étais pas aussi licencieuse.
Tu barbouilles l'écusson antiseptique des marchands
tu sâlis les souliers qui avancent dans la boutique
enduis de ton empreinte
empuant l'air
conditionné à grands frais.

Tu es une souillon qui tombe ses jupes en dérision
alors que les citoyens convenables doivent passer
aussi délicatement qu'en marchant sur des oeufs
bien qu'ils ne puissent que désirer, du magasin,
des préservatifs.

Et, Ginko, chérie, je te donne raison
mais ne peux l'avouer.

Ton petit fruit plein d'espoir, je l'ai pris
tandis qu'ils emportaient tes crottes
c'était rond,
froid,
intègre,
dans ma main, pitoyable
je le déposai un moment, avec révérence, sur le toit d'une
                                         Porsche blanche
pour mieux l'admirer.

Après quoi, je n'eus que le choix
d'emplir furtivement mes poches
de tes ambitions survivantes
m'asseoir dans le bus dans ta peste
— mes rougeurs interrompant la dormance hivernale de tes
                                         semences —
jusqu'à un endroit convenable à la rivière
où je les ai plantées pour toi
Ginko, femme chérie.

(Trans. Mireille Harnett)

Ogham

Bhí mo chroí ag cur dathanna de gur tháinig tú -
dath-ogham
d'fhéadfá a rá —
ag insint uaignis
nó áthas
nó éagmais
mar a d'oir.

Dathanna contrártha
anuas ar a chéile go minic
is an scuab gan scóip.

Ach ar do theacht
d'fhigh na dathanna ar fad
mar urlár romhat
is tháinig tú i dtír
le cúpla stróic dath-ghlan
a Oghma ghrianainigh.

Ogham

Mon coeur changeait constamment de couleurs jusqu'à ton
arrivée,
Un Ogham de couleurs,
tu pourrais dire
racontant la solitude
ravissement
ou désir
selon le cas.

Des couleurs choquantes
toutes entrevêchées souvent,
le pinceau manquant de verve.

Mais lorsque tu arrivas
toutes les couleurs se fusionnèrent
comme un fond pour toi
et tu vins
en quelques coups de pinceaux nets et colorés
Oghma ghrianainigh.

(Trans. Mireille Harnett)

125

Sara Berkeley

Valley Poem I

I was not built for
The dull rumble of the valley air,
The great steel birds
That fly with a dark grey
Whine, grazing the sky.
They fly low in the blue face of it
They spell out its naked state,
The clouds are at bay.

The fault sniggers beneath the highway,
She cracks her knuckles publicly
But keeps apart her joy
Narrow and deep; some day
She will send a flame
From the scorched well of the earth
And burn off the teeming human layer,
She will burst her corset of rock
And take the air,
She needs room, she was not meant
For the brittle rib-cage of the bay.

Valley Poem II

Wherever you look
She answers back
You know her by the jewels
Set shallow and close for eyes
That narrow
And are never shrewd.
You know her by the good bones,
The many thoughts that fall on gold,
Her families are few
Or they hide; her smile is broad
While out of the bullets of fast cars
She builds a war,
Under their hail of horns
Only such surface gestures can be made -
The nod, the solemn wave,
When there is call to celebrate
Her laughter is canned,
A cast of hawks falls on her parade,
I know her for a young girl,
Virginal, pure,
You skin your knuckles
Trying to knock some love from her.

Convalescent

There's smoke in the air although it's spring,
People are shedding muddy boots and things,
Slamming their private doors
On rooms with sofas and TVs,
I fall into the wind
It rights me, mildly,
And I walk like a convalescent
Down a tree-lined path,
Wood-soothed, thinking of bough
And bark and all that will come
Of the nutshell,
The circles in the circles
That the lathe handles lovingly
With its gaze
The hacked limb a lumberman heals
With his dab of bright paint.
Somewhere friends are waiting,
Lies in their hands,
Hands by their sides.

Evelyn Conlon

On The Inside Of Cars

It was the beginning of a long weekend and long weekends can be lonely, or good, or dangerous. The children were going by sea with their father to visit their paternal grandparents. Chrissie got up early to do dreadful things, commit sacrifices to an image that she had never even wanted. But she would prove to them that she could have children with polished shoes and matching clothes. Before she woke them, she had early morning sickness not only from too little sleep and too many cigarettes, but as a monument to her motherhood. Having once learned the relief of contracting her stomach muscles, she could do it now at will and so throw herself better at the day ahead. She didn't fit her hand into the shoes, as she blacked, marooned and browned them, because her hand was too big. Blue shirt navy blue jumper and denim for the eldest, pale yellow shirt dark green jumper and denim for the red haired, the difficult one, white shirt rust jumper and denim for her favourite. They ate breakfast then, — the older two trying, out of remarkable sensitivity, not to be too excited, the younger one bungling his way right through his mother's heart. She brushed their hairs, that had given her varying degrees of heartburn, and let them fall whatever way they wanted. Black eiderdown, red razors, and brown feathery curls. She was a great one for love. She wished he would come soon so she could stop her hands from being involuntary instruments of care and let them hold her own breasts. He did. She answered the door to tidiness. Of course, she didn't look at him but from the corner of her eye she could see ten years of her life and she could smell clean living. He chatted this particular morning because he must have forgotten who she was. She took the children to the cleanest car she would ever now see and filed them into the back seat. He was checking the front lamp. Her whole body leaned into his property. She settled them all comfortably, all of them, even the young one, quiet, — looking at her delighted that she was also doing this. She was nearly overcome by clean car smell, the soft music from perfect speakers, not a wire out of place, the dust free comfort, as in the cars of rich people or young men excited with their purchase. She moved their clothes, moved them, rearranged, so she could smell this for longer. She could go away on a date in a car like this. Jesus, Chrissie, where are your political morals? Just for comfort. She pulled her body and life out of the stale success, waved goodbye and said well, now you're free Chrissie. Do. Do. She had not relearned yet that people were allowed minutes or days to make plans. She stepped inside. The house was a space, enclosed of function with nothing to function about. A god Crazy came into her soul and she went to the boat to peep-tom on her own children and their father, parking the car and leaving the island.

She did not look like a woman who was hiding and she placed herself for the perfect view of the people and the matters such as were her concern now. A man and children passed before her. The man was not talking to the children because he was organising tickets, safety and time. The children tottered behind him, plodding aimlessly onto the boat, not sure of what navigation meant. Those were her children.

Excuse me, sir - those children there. They grew to outrageous sizes in my womb and split my body open in order to get out. In time, my body healed a little. Now they break my heart but it's my cunt that cries. That man with them was my husband. He was, I suppose still is, English and a class up from me on top of that. We went on our honeymoon to see his parents. Can you imagine that for a honeymoon? Mind you, I was dying to see his parents because of the romance. He hadn't told them that he was getting married, so I was welcomed first as a nice Irish friend, then I went outside to the apple blossom while he told them his news. It had nothing to do with me. They and him then brought me in and gave me tea, welcoming me, I suppose, as a wife (which I hated), his mother shocked but still she gave me sympathetic looks. The sleeping arrangements were changed with the heavy-footedness that should be reserved only for funerals. It was a cruel thing to do to her but I went along with it because I was dazzled by him and hadn't grown up. How desperate, how terrible, sir, that there is not even a nod of friendship left after all that dazzlement.

One of the men in suits looked at her - he could have sworn that she was talking to herself. She wore a black coat and a golden scarf. Her eyes pierced holes in her heart. That time, her parents-in-law — the first time the law had any bearing on her life — took a photo of them, her and their son. She couldn't remember which of the parents had held the camera. She had worn a machine-knit cardigan that reached to her knees and had a four-inch waist band. The sister of a woman at work had knit it along with hundreds of others and had made a fortune. She then got a brain tumour and died. These facts were there immovable from her memory. Facts were such harsh things. They could not be changed. Not even the frills of them could be turned about to make it easier. His mother had fussed a little but then got to like her. Chrissie. Rather a strange name. His young sister had said that she had two chins. It was a good honeymoon she thought, although she had nothing to compare it with.

They had come back and moved into a house that he had found. Her heart was nearly crushed by the symmetry of the street. It took her months to know which house was hers. She talked about this as if it was what it indeed was, the greatest crime committed against her to date. But it was only a beginning. In no time at all, she was a dormitory sleeper giving out breast milk and sex. The men ran out of houses into the morning into cars and zoomed away to life, glad to be out of that mêlée for a while. She wore a dressing gown late and tried to sleep her life away with the babies. Sometimes he said, "You can have the car, I don't need it today" and she let it sit there in the garage because she had nowhere to go -with babies. On those days she sometimes fingered the car keys absently.

There he was now on the way up the gang plank. There they were, her babies being led away like lambs to people they didn't know, because of the law. That red hair was her brother's.

When she said she was leaving "this good house" to go live in a dump he said, "Not with my children, you're not." "Yes I am" she said, "and they're my children."

She had a point. Then he said that none of the children were his. This was a man's privilege, they are, they aren't, they are, they aren't. So she said, "Yes, they are all your children."

These days he kept telling each of them how like himself they were. Panic, she presumed. They were gone into the stomach of the boat and she could do nothing now but be free.

This holiday, he intended to wipe her out for a week. His parents would not mention her and gradually the children would stop talking of her because they would learn that they got no response. He would bring them to clean places, his father's car would be spotless and Chrissie's favourite would long for the hole in her uncle's car, that his mother sometimes borrowed, through which he could see the road. Chrissie's favourite would also think that they didn't even want him to talk about her, but what else was there to talk about? He would become quiet. Chrissie's husband had ideas about how to get rid of her out of her children's heads - all of these ideas taking as their central point money, tidiness and other states related to tidiness. Surely if he showed them the proper way to live they would forget about her, with her unabashed poverty, her steeliness in the face of what they would not have had to suffer if she'd behaved herself. But would they forget her dreams? He would try. This holiday he would try.

Chrissie heard him thinking hate down the gang plank through the waiting room and into her bones. Still, she could hardly complain — in her bitterer days she had passed through a town where he'd brought them once. They had previously told her about it with a hushed excitement. Now she was going through this town on a train, unexpectedly. The name jumped at her and hit her in the stomach. She frantically talked to all three of them at the same time, gorging them into her, so that they wouldn't become distracted by him. On the way back she relented and they smiled at her, one long single smile, for remembering. She had looked out the window far away, far far away, letting her eyes fill up again, the name of the town giving her a headache. She walked away from the pier. The woman in the black coat and the golden scarf, with her hands in her pockets fidgeting for the need of something between them, a blanket, a pan or a child.

Sir, if only I hadn't had them. Can you imagine how I would look, how I would be? If you can, you've a better imagination than me. And maybe it's not imagination you've got because, after all, I do remember not having them - do remember me. You don't even know me now nor then. Still, they're not really children, they're my children. Indeed you're right sir, they would have had, could have had a different life if I had not been foolish. But who are you to say that I am a saleable life to be traded against what you call a normal home? My next door neighbours' son - eighteen - was a vegetarian. His father, one Sunday, cornered him and tried to force meat down his throat. I heard the screams but thought that they could not possibly be on our street. It changed my mind about normality.

Another man in another suit could have sworn that the woman said something to him. No sir, I'm afraid I didn't speak to you. She swung past him her face showing a brilliant contempt. Contempt like that was living art.

Sir, she thought, if only I hadn't had them I could go now, go and be gone when he came back and never have to see him again, which is after all what the whole thing was about. My babies. My poor dear babies. How could I think them out of existence. Once, though, I bumped into my husband on the street. We both nearly stopped, forgetting for a split second the last seven years, not remembering for a tiny flash that we hated each other. We said hello because it was too late not to, then we sprang as if burned, up the street in opposite directions, which is the way we should always have been going. I thought sorrow, vengeance, then pity - for me who couldn't go, stuck on an island full of catholics because of a husband. Sir.

When Chrissie got home she noticed the dead crocuses. They lay flat in the window boxes like purple, yellow and white snail's slime.

Because such blackness does not have survivors to tell tales, Chrissie woke next morning on Sunday with a new approach floating in her dreams. She went walking in the park, wearing a red jacket, a silver scarf, and carelessly twiddling a daffodil. But the park was full of men with children. Men who ten years previously would have been in pubs at this time, drinking their Sunday morning pint before going home to the dinner and the wife. Now they were embarrassedly running around after the children, putting them awkwardly on swings, exercising their access rights. She had never been that fond of parks but today this one was particularly bad, even worse than normal - it had become the exchange point. Mostly mischievous children, who knew when big people had had it up to there, and some serious, hardened children, were passed from one sullen parent to another. In that brief moment, the big people each tried to hold on to dignity, self-righteousness and contempt - poor excuses for what was once love. The mischievous children took advantage of the moment before being whipped into line by the receiving parent who didn't wish to appear out of control. Chrissie sidled out of the park as if it had nothing to do with her and she was just a normal, Sunday morning woman thinking about lust. At the bus stop a child had well and truly got the better of her father - she was eight, he was forty.

"I'm going to tell Mammy."

"Fucking tell your Mammy whatever you like. You just do that." You'd think he was talking to a six footer.

"Yes. Just do that."

He caught his chest.

"She has me heart broke. Her effen mother, excuse the language, has her ruined."

Chrissie's approach for positivity was getting buffeted on the outside so she headed for home again. She passed two ugly teenage boys and heard them talking about the lack of talent at their school. Naturally she let it go - they weren't hers.

Why couldn't she have put up with it - what was so difficult about one house, one man. She'd done everything else for him, sat on a chair one night, thinking just that, feeling an intrauterine device sear through her insides up to her tonsils. It was only supposed to be for the lower, the dangerous, regions but it left its pains in every other part of her body too. The doctor had talked about politics as she embedded the foreign object in her pink womb. This helped Chrissie not to think of the mutilation and the pain. When she had met him first, she had gone to bed a lot between letters, taking their love with her and hiding it under the blankets, even wrapping it up inside her so no one could steal it from her. How more faithful could she have been. She had rung his telephone number even when she knew he wasn't there, just to hear it ring. Hadn't she had children for him? For him. Certainly it could not have been for herself. How much more could she have done? In the first year, when they fought, she said she was sorry, always sorry, and meant it. Later, when they fought, she put her arms tight around the baby and made an outsider of him. It was her only possible defence against the words of a healthy man. They walked home one time, she pleading for a taxi as her monthly blood seeped from her insides, he, with the money in his pocket, refusing. He thought that she would forget that. Chrissie found it hard to remember now the love that must have been there. Every time love screamed at her, or the memory of it, she ran, as train passengers do who do not want to watch the flickering time boards. She had written a message for him once on a dusty bus, that much she did allow herself to think upon.

"If you pass here you'll have walked the same steps as me. Love Chrissie."

When he had got the divorce papers, she was raging that she hadn't thought of it first, or even had one procured, and she could have said, "You moron, I did that years ago." He would have got the papers in a serious fashion, she could just see him, as if cutting out something distasteful. She would have done it in style and gone for wine afterwards.

Her children. Where were they now? Liking the sea she hoped. Not afraid, she hoped. Last week the middle one had said "We have this couch in our father's, you can make a bed out of it."

"Do you indeed and is it black leather and does it have a silver spring and is the shape of a pregnant woman's supine body branded on it?

"What did you say Mammy?"

"Nothing."

"And we have this tape."

"Really. And is there a song on it called 'Make me an island?' Ha!"

"How did you know that?"

She slammed the door, my couch and again - my tape. By Jesus, wait until your twenty first. See that corner. I'm going to get you into it and tell you about your precious father. I wouldn't do it for a while, ten or fifteen years or so, because I'd be afraid of mentally deranging you or giving you a complex. What I do to save your mental health and your ego. But it will keep. This corner here. And you'll know then from where I got this tight lip that gets tighter by the month. This corner. That is, if we're still in this flat.

On Sundays, before and after the first was born but not after the second, they used to go visiting. Sunday morning loveliness first, reminiscent in its own way of polished shoes and purity. Sex somewhere between twelve and two. Dinner before or after. Never as good as mother's. Not even once. Then fear would descend upon her. The weekend was over now - Sunday afternoon could not offer any opium, any panacea. Monday isolation looming and she wouldn't see anyone for another week. So she would inveigle him to go visiting, on the pretext that a drive would be good after their love making. He wanted to sleep. First year, they would head equally either for C and R's or P and K's - next year they headed more often for P and K's because P had a baby too. Third year, equal again because R had a child now. C and R were different than P and K in smallish ways, not in any major way that one expects from our belief that the individual is unique. (Not to mention the set of two individuals.) C and R bought a dearer suite of furniture but P and K spent what they saved by buying the plastic suite on a superior three-in-one set. Both C and R and P and K bought dining-room suites, washing machines and do-it-themselves combinations on/in which to store their wedding presents. Chrissie would sit dazed. She never knew the difference between makes of food mixers and was deficient in her knowledge of woods. Should they have stayed at home? Perhaps if they had, C and R or P and K might have visited them in the way that young frightened married couples will drop in on each other to check that things have not gone too far wrong. At least in her own home, she could have had some control over the conversation.

"When is the baby due, Chrissie?"

"What baby?"

She felt her womb and pretended she'd thought it was someone else they were asking her about.

"Sorry, me oh me, eh, four months."

Whose house was she in? Was it C and R's or P and K's? They would then drive home, or rather her husband would drive home and she would look out the window at Sunday visitors who had been out looking for people like themselves, some of them successful, some of them unsuccessful, missing, passing the people they were looking for on both journeys as they - the people they were looking for - looked for them and missed, passed them. She hadn't seen C and R or P and K since. Wonder what they were like now. Would she have even one word to say to them? Probably one hundred and sixteen Sunday afternoons. Each.

Her children would be there by now.

"Daddy's taking us to IngaLand. Why do you never take us there, Mammy?"

Silence. There were three possible answers to that and then the real one. She opted for silence.

Once they had gone to a hotel to meet some or other manager. She sat on the soft seat looking at the glass doors, at cars and porters, at excitement, at sex, at beauty. He ranted and railed about privilege, about class. Who was he to talk? She knew nothing about these things, only about freedom. A manager or other joined them - she still looked out the glass doors - lights, car lights, were coming on - cheating the summer night of awesomeness. The excitement was getting hotter.

"What did you say Chrissie?"

"Sorry, nothing. Excuse me I must go to —" Jesus, the toilets were fit for living in, still, they were only toilets. Freshen your mouth right now. 20p. for a prepasted tooth-brush. Imagine. She hoped she had two tens. She did. How could she remember it, that brush? It was blue plastic with a screw-on top, plastic brush, a smell of fresh toothpaste. It was travel, travel bags, trains, talking to strangers, new cities, flat hot countries, mirages. She put it in her bag for when she would need it. It was that, and that sort of thing, which made her leave "this good house" "the good house" "your home". The fool forgot for a moment in the saying of it that she had three children, and by then it was too late. Still, they were the only mistake she hadn't made. Her time would come.

"You're forcing me to consider hitting you.'

That was worse, only in some senses, than being hit. She waited to be hit. She never was, just starved. But her time would come some day for revenge.

By the time of the actual split she was so tired that all she ever thought of was sleep. The split itself wasn't such a big thing to her at all. As things had deteriorated to a noticeable level, relations started calling on her, during the day - anything to stop the whole thing from falling apart. Anything. At least she wasn't on her own any more. Maybe if they'd done it sooner? She wished she had the nerve to ask them to let her go to bed for a short sleep, just a little sleep, instead of talking to her. Immediately they'd come in the door she'd think of her bed. Remember that Sunday they'd joined the queue of parking cars outside the church, like any other suburban couple, with the country mother in the front seat beside the man, the driver, the daughter or daughter-in-law in the back. When the rumpus erupted because they'd missed mass - the times had been changed six months before - Chrissie was fast asleep. The sun streamed in on her and despite the annoyance, they left her - her mother nearly sympathetic, despite the mass problem.

She decided to clean the house, always better than remembering and it came natural to her by now, but she knew it was daft to do house work when she wasn't confined. Yet what could she do? In the end, she used the long weekend to feel sorry for herself, with good reason, (it was also therapeutic and it saved her from feeling inadequate) and the rest of the week to become a new Chrissie yet again. She talked to herself, went for walks dressed in white, black, purple, told secrets to the one tree in the street, and kicked expensive cars on her way home at night. By the time they came back, half of her wanted to squeeze radiance into their faces, another half would have passed them in the street and pretended it had run away from home. But her favourite smiled first and that settled that.

Medbh McGuckian

The Horse Fair

If days could speak the names within them,
My watch hanging on a branch would be
A combination of reopened wind. But trees
Do not detach themselves during leaves,
The air circulates in the near-white crawl
Spaces, I touch the unfallen sky as an instrument.

Between every two moments stands a daughter,
A dark or bright cloud with inrolling border,
And after its repeated breakage the cloudflow
Stops abruptly. For more than an hour a blaze
Of strong and heavy blue, bearded, unbearded,
Then bearded again, forces its face of light
Like death or the first small scarlet kiss
Bringing your once-born face your own face.

The "Esther Sleepe"

In the tongue of summer a vessel was becalmed:
Some not yet over storm had burned her to a cinder
That outshone the crust of starfish
She took no umbrage from.

Was that her novel, to be written out,
Like one with every wearable, keeping
a room ready and aired for un homme
Comme il y en a peu?

"To a lady, with some Painted Flowers" -
Past forgiving anyone, she crashed,
She fell, stones in her governed arms
Had house-keeping thoughts.

The Unplayed Rosalind

July presides, light with a boy's hat,
Dressed in black with his feet on a cushion,
His voice-print is too dry for the stage.

The long-stemmed flowers comparatively
Rained, and the tumultuous sea was making me
Sterile, as though a hand from within it
Slowly drove me back, we were small objects
On its edge.

The telegraph pole sang because a horseshoe
Brushed its foot, and a spider's web darkened
On my finger like a kiss that has to be paid
With the veil lowered, a sweet-sour kiss through tight
Bitten lips that could make me drunk.

I have lived on a war footing and slept
On the blue revolution of my sword;
Given the perfect narrative nature of blue,
I have been the poet of women and consequently
Of the young, if you burned my letters
In the soiled autumn they would form two hearts.

The room which I thought the most beautiful
In the world, and never showed to anyone,
Is a rose-red room, a roseate chamber,
It lacks two windowpanes and has no waterjug.
There is red ink in the inkwell.

Upstairs above my head lives someone
Who repeats my movements with her double
Weeping. My heart beats as though it were
Hers, and sometimes I have her within my clothes
Like a blouse fastened with a strap.

She moved in her dream, she lost her dream,
She stretched her arms and tossed her head
As a river burrows its bed till the bed burns.
Her dress reminded me of curtains torn
Like a page from a bedroom window.

There was a rustle in the lock of the door,
A noise like grasshoppers as though a great
Moth were caught in it. Then the door
Simply waved, and a long white sheet
Of paper came gliding from under it,
Like a coaster shoved beneath everyone's
Wineglass, or glass being cut under water.

In her there was something of me which
He touched, when she lay on his arm like the unknown
Echo of the word I wanted to hear
Only from his mouth, she spoke words to him
I had already heard.

She said, "This is too bright for me",
Preferring to see the firered rip down heaven
As a saucer of iced water where she could
Dip her hands, as in the reciprocal blue
Ashes of his eyes.

She kissed him as if he were her child
Like a gull rubbing its beak against
A jagged window, and my body felt
All its gossip's knots being traced.

She removed the rose from my mouth
Like the taste of fruit or a button left
On the top of a cupboard. Though she swore
That she did not carry
Another man's child under her heart,
My seed is a loose stormcoat
Of gold silk, with wide sleeves, in her uterus.

Éilís Ní Dhuibhne

The Wife of Bath

It is a fact universally acknowledged that organised group trips
are not a type of amusement calculated to appeal to the tastes of
the discriminating tourist, whatever their benefits for anyone
else ... and I doubt if they are many. My own attitude to such
excursions has always been one of scorn and detestation. And
this feeling I have extended to all related activities, such as
christmas parties and end of term socials, ever since I was a
pupil at the Convent of the Broken Heart, Rathgar, when my
most acute torture was the weekly hop. This was organised,
under keen supervision, by the kind sisters and their brethren in
an adjacent and utterly respectable boys" school, attended by
thoroughly rude and wild young cads. In spite of the presence
of a nun in every corner and one or two Christian brothers on
the stage, sharing the duty of mc between them, the hops had
been occasions of the greatest vulgarity, noise and vanity, as far
as I was concerned. I attended only because Mother, then in her
heyday, full of the joys of living and happy as a lark with dear
Daddy, insisted that I should.

"It's natural for young people to go out and have a good
time!" she would cry, in response to my weak protests. "All work
and no play makes Jill a dull girl!"

That I loved work and hated play seemed only to fuel her
enthusiasm for the school hop. She has always had my best
interests at heart, dear Mother, and, assuming that she could
have no inkling of the true nature of the event, I submitted to
her wishes. What could she, extrovert and lovely, have known of
the pain which the event caused me, her clumsy misbegotten
daughter? But for her sake I endured it, and other equally
unsavoury festivities, until I did the Leaving examination. Then
I rewarded myself with the freedom to organise my own social
life, if not any other aspect of my existence, and allowed myself
the pleasure of foregoing absolutely all forms of artificial
conviviality. And except for the time when I was courted by
Paddy ... a passage which is best forgotten ... I have continued
this particular form of abstinence to the present day. So when
the teacher at my evening class in basic Italian urged us all to

take a coach to England for the October bank holiday weekend, I immediately turned a deaf ear to his entreaties: I have a special and truly useful gift of being able to stop hearing whenever it is really necessary, and to devote my attention to my private thoughts and ideas. The teacher ... his name was Rory, he was not a real Italian ... had been prattling on for some minutes, filling in valuable teaching time with nonsense about tickets and deposits, when, through my haze of memories and associations, the word *Bath* suddenly penetrated with the clarity of a foghorn. Immediately, I was aroused from my reverie and possessed by a compelling desire to break the habit of twenty years. And go. Because Bath, which I had never visited, meant so much to me.

The very word, small and plain as it is, rolled around my mouth, smooth as ivory. What a deliciously English word it is: Bath. The *a* is a test, the *th* the trial that tells the sheep from the goats, the cultured from the masses, the old from the nouveau and, let me admit it, the English from us. Aloud, I could not myself pronounce it as it ought to be uttered without feeling pretentious. With my mind's tongue, however, I can say it with panache and pleasure, give it all the beauty which its elegant long vowel, its rich consonantal cluster, call for.

But however much I savoured the sound of the name, it was the place itself, or what it conjured up for me, that drew me to it. And what was that, if not Jane Austen. Jane Austen, and her works, and her characters. If they were not all set in Bath all of the time, it was Bath which suited them best as a backdrop, it was Bath which was, for me, the quintessential Austen place.

And Jane Austen has been my favourite writer ever since I was a girl of nine, sitting at my mother's knee by the fire in our house in Rathmines: the house in which I still reside, but then so much more alive and so much more filled with gaiety and warmth, when Mother was in her heyday and Daddy was with us! It was Mother who introduced me to the novels, reading from abridged versions, of lively Elizabeth and placid Fanny, of sensible Elinor and patient Anne, of delightfully ordinary Catherine Morland — and of all the eccentric, domineering, maddening old fogies: Mrs Bennet and Mrs Jennings, Lady Catherine de Burgh and Mrs Ferrars! How we would laugh, Mother and I, at their tricks and foibles! How we admired Catherine for her innocence, Elinor for her common sense, in overcoming their schemes and confounding the consequences of their folly! How we ignored the men, idle, unreliable, skittish as the best were, bounders as the rest were! Could such men have existed, we might have asked, but did not. They did. They still did, and we knew it, both of us, all too well, in spite of Daddy and his goodness. But Daddy and his goodness deserted us in the end, too. When I was sixteen he had a stroke and died. Not his fault, of course, but typical of his sex.

Yes, I would go to Bath, on the college trip. It was not the ideal mode, but fate had thrown it in my path, and I knew if I did not accept its challenge, the opportunity to go on this pilgrimage which I had, I realised now, waited for since I was nine, would probably not come my way again.

My single regret was that Mother, who had shared my love for Austen, could not accompany me.

But she was not a student at the college, and, more significantly, she has been almost, although never quite, bedridden, for the past ten years. It is as a result of this fact that I so seldom take a holiday of any kind. A long weekend, however, and to such a place, would not be out of the question. I would make all the necessary arrangements. Mother would not suffer.

So I expected her to be as enthusiastic as I was about my little plans. To my surprise, she was not.

"Isn't it late in the year for holidays?" she asked, her lined face taking on an ancient exhausted look: sometimes Mother can look a thousand years old.

"Well, a bit, perhaps," I replied cheerfully. "But the weather is often at its best in October. And you know how fond I am of the autumn colours!"

"It's dark at five," she continued as if I had not spoken. Mother shares with me the gift of voluntary deafness.

"Six," I retorted, too sharply. It is not always easy to be patient with Mother, and I owe her such a lot! "Alasdair and Betty will bring you over to Bray for the weekend: it'll be a break for you, and it's all arranged. They're delighted to have you!"

This was untrue. "Alasdair, my only brother, had been far from co-operative, but for once I'd put my foot down. Even if Betty had a Writers' Workshop and little Fiach was teething, I felt he owed this weekend to me. After all, I had minded Mother for approximately seven hundred and fifty weekends, without a great deal of reward or, let me be frank, gratitude, from him. And I did so want to go to Bath.

So I went.

I got up early the morning after our arrival at an hotel some miles to the south of Bath; thus I avoided any meeting with members of the Rathmines Tour, who had, I gathered, spent most of the previous night dancing in a discotheque at an adjacent public house, The Hop Pole Inn. A bus — taxis in Bath are rather expensive — took me to the city centre, and there my holiday really began: I walked along Beau Nashe's terraces, I traced the path of Catherine Morland and Isabel Thorpe along Pultney Street, I examined the great medieval Abbey, I was suitably astonished by the steamy Roman baths with their carvings of goddesses and heaps of ancient coins. Finally, I entered the Pump Room, where Austen had so often sat and taken the waters, where Catherine had strolled around in circles, waiting in vain for Mr Tilney. They served tea there now, made on the famous water, and I treated myself to a cup, since the surroundings were so enchanting in their associations and, indeed, in their ornament. From finest china I sipped my beverage, listening with gratification to the clink of silver spoons and the lilt of received pronunciation. The restaurant was filled with delightful old ladies ... everyone in Bath seemed to be at least sixty. Their faces were peachy and delicate, they seemed to be dressed uniformly in the best of discreet good taste: beige twinsets, lacy blouses of snow white linen abounded. I bathed in the atmosphere, tea and conversation, so much more congenial than the somewhat pagan aura of the baths themselves — interesting they certainly were, but their steamy atmosphere, their naked statues, were not to my taste — Austen does not often refer to them. Perhaps she does not refer to them at all. And I am quite sure she never plunged in: bathing is such a vulgar habit really, I have always avoided it myself. One is so messy afterwards. Taking the waters, or, even better, taking tea, is another matter altogether, and here in the Pump Room there was no trace of mess. All was ordered, genteel, nice. I eavesdropped on the couple at the table next to mine, vaguely hoping that they might be discussing literature. But no: they seemed to be intent on comparing house prices in Bath and London. Turning my attention to the other side, I was dismayed to find that the people at that table, two old women with the faces of porcelain dolls, were avidly describing a very sadistic murder which had recently been committed in Limpley Stoke ... the suburb in which my hotel was located.

I swallowed my tea and, feeling suddenly tired, returned to the latter.

None of the members of the Rathmines Adult Education Institute were there: they had gone in their coach to lunch in an inn near Stonehenge, the receptionist told me, and I felt a sudden twinge of disappointment. I did not like my companions much, and would have preferred to make the acquaintance of the native population. But although the residents of Bath were all very nobly spoken, none of them had spoken to me. I would have welcomed the opportunity to exchange a few remarks, banal as they would surely be, with anyone, even a person from

Dublin. The hotel staff was not talkative. My attempts to engage the receptionist in conversation came to nought: she nodded, and smiled, then bent her fair-haired head over a Sunday supplement and ignored me.

Disgruntled, I decided to go for a walk by the River Avon, which flowed along majestically just below the hotel. True, the description of the murder lingered unpleasantly in my mind, but it was broad daylight, and I did not plan to venture far. Besides, I was obliged to pass the afternoon in some way, and felt quite a strong reluctance to go into town again immediately.

The river bank was wooded and provided with a bridle path: at least, a signpost said that that was what it was. Crunching crisp leaves underfoot, I proceeded on my way, planning to walk a mile or so and then turn back. Perhaps I would try Bath again, in the evening. Perhaps, at a more tranquil time of day, I would find what I had so far failed to discover in its graceful streets and expensive shops: the true spirit of Jane Austen. Thus I mused, as I walked along, enjoying to the full the cold of the afternoon, cold which seemed to be rising from the deep, rich-smelling clay, and which was curiously relieved by the roar of the river. Ah yes. Jane Austen. Had I expected too much? One town, one trip, one weekend, could not have delivered all that. And what was it I had expected? I do not know.

Suddenly, lost in thought as I was, a loud crash interrupted me, and caused me to jump. It came from somewhere in the trees. I walked a little in its direction, and beheld, on the ground, a very fat woman, picking mud and leaves from her clothes and meanwhile grumbling at a huge placid horse, who stood nearby and nibbled grass, quite unconcerned at the abuse which was being heaped upon his imbecilic head.

"Are you all right?" I asked, by way of introduction.

"Of course I'm not all right," the individual replied. "I've just fallen off that stupid beast, I'm black and blue all over." And she shook her head angrily.

This action effected the release of a red scarf, which she had tied over her hair. It fell to the ground, and a cloud of yellow, blatantly peroxide, curls, sprang out around her face, which was round, plump and raddled, possibly from the exertion which she had undergone, or possibly, more probably, permanently.

"Come here, Scott," she addressed the horse in milder tones, and I noted a strong Somerset accent, of the type possessed by Postman Pat, a character with whom I am familiar thanks to the Sunday afternoons I occasionally spend in the company of Alasdair's children.

The horse raised his head knowingly and ambled slowly up to

her. She tried to mount him but fell back from the stirrup with a cry: "Bloody hell! Ouch!"

"Can I be of some assistance?" I asked rhetorically, since I could not envisage helping someone who seemed to be at least twice my weight (I weigh ten stones, ten and a half when I am not careful, nine and three quarters when I am lucky).

"Doubt it!" she said. "I think it'll be shank's mare for the moment. Which way are you going?"

"Well," I pondered, "Which way are you going?"

"Right along this here path, as far as the Hop Pole Inn," she replied. "Coming with me?"

"I happen to be going in that direction myself."

She was unspeakably vulgar: dressed most unsuitably in a denim overall and pink anorak, brilliant red socks showing at the edge of her boots; loudmouthed and foul mouthed, with a country accent of the cheapest kind. But I felt drawn to her. Everything about her, even her weight, was positive and appealing: she reminded me of the kind of fertility goddess I had not seen represented at the Roman baths, but which belonged there.

"You on holiday hereabouts, then?""Well yes, I am," I admitted, ashamed, as always, to acknowledge tourist status.

"Wouldn't be my own choice," she said. "Give me Italy. Or Turkey. Or Israel even. But everyone to her fancy, and me to my Nancy, as the old woman said when she kissed the cow."

"I'm interested in the literary associations of the town," I offered this rather hopelessly.

"Oh!" she replied, and began to nudge Scott again.

"Jane Austen and all that, you know," I went on lamely.

"Jane Austen! Never heard of her!"

"She wrote novels."

"Wrote what? I never did hear of a woman who could write! My husband, one of them, was it Jankyn? I can't rightly remember now. He wrote all the time, and a bloody waste of time it was too. The only thing he was interested in was writing about women, and how evil they were! My God, I used to tell him, if women wrote I know what they'd write about men: all kinds of wickedness, I should warrant! Jankyn just laughed, he did, when I told him that! Said women were so naturally stupid they could never learn anything half as complicated as writing! Silly Jankyn! Or was it Piers? Lots of 'em played that game, my husbands, they were always scratching away if they got half a chance. Anything's better than honest work, what?"

She scratched her mop of hair, and I sidled away a bit.

"You've been married more than once?"

She guffawed.

"More than once? I been married five times at the very least. Five, ten, a hundred ... don't ask me how often I've been married. More often than you've eaten hot dinners, I reckon."

"How interesting," I murmured.

"It were surely interesting ... men are interesting, you know, as objects of ... study. They're like different kinds of plants ... or wild animals. One of my husbands, I think it was the sixth or the seventh, was really interested in them. He had a big book full of pictures of all kinds of beasts, griffins and unicorns and elephants and phoenixes and I don't know what. Half of them never seen the light of day, I used to tell him, but he wouldn't believe me, oh no, he was always right. And I was always wrong, on account of being so stupid, you understand."

"Hmm. Why did you keep on marrying, if they were all so ... so..."

"Violent, penny-pinching, drunk, foolish, unfaithful, nagging, boring ... That's what they were. Well, why, I wonder? What else could I have done? I liked to use my instrument, you see, I did like that, I always have done and I still do. That was one reason ..."

"You play the piano ... or something?"

"No!" she gave me a sharp look, and then exchanged a rather knowing one with Scott. "I never was good at playing anything like that. Sewing, that was my hobby. I was certainly a dab hand at embroidery, everyone said that much about me!"

"And you married five husbands ..."

"More!"

"More than five, in order to do embroidery?"

"Oh for Christ's sake! Shall I spell it out? I married them for sex, first of all, and secondly for money. Let's face it, I had no choice, how else could I have lived?"

"Sewing?"

"No woman has ever made a decent living from sewing. Ask anyone who's tried it ... no, marriage beats sewing hands down, and it's better for your health ... it has disadvantages, mind, I'm the first to admit it. Hell, does it have disadvantages!"

She guffawed again, although why I did not know.

"One long battle, that's what marriage is!"

"Oh, now, surely there are many exceptions to that!"

"You know of any?" she seemed genuinely surprised.

"Well, my parents, for instance, were always very happy."

Mother and Daddy. A marriage made in heaven. Never a cross word. Daddy always did exactly what Mother wished — except his last act, except for dying. But until then he was her willing slave.

"No need to ask who wore the pants, if they were happy. But I always tried to make sure I did too, it's the only way. Ever been married yourself?"

"No, not exactly," I blushed: such a personal question!

"What do you mean, not exactly?"

"Once I was ... engaged."

To Paddy. A long time ago ... but I remember it as if it were yesterday. Faithless Paddy. No integrity, no class. An arts student, on a grant: a mechanic's son from Crumlin. "Really!" Mother had said, laughing quietly into her handkerchief when he came to tea. "How nice!" She did not pass him the sandwiches, or show him to the door when he was leaving. That time, or on his three subsequent visits. Whenever I mentioned him, she changed the subject. She had my best interests at heart. She saw through him from the beginning. "We all sow our wild oats!" she would laugh, as I prepared for my dates. "Youth must have its fling!" She was right about Paddy. After four months he left me, standing under Clery's clock. "Stood me up" is the expression, I believe. I never saw him again after that, but heard he had gone to England, to take up a teaching position there.

"It's not the same thing at all. I've never been engaged, not even once, but I've been married ..."

"More than five times. Yes I know. So what's so special about that? I've seen lots of marriages, I've observed them from the outside. Just like Jane Austen did."

"Jane who? Sorry, I'm a bit deaf sometimes?"

"Austen. She lived here once. I've mentioned her already: she wrote novels, all about marriage ... or more precisely, about getting a husband."

"That's a different thing entirely, isn't it? Shouldn't be surprised if she'd been engaged too, but not married."

"She wasn't."

"There, you see, I knew it ... she didn't know anything about men, no more than Saint Jerome and all those old chaps Jankyn was always going on about knew about women. All twaddly in the poddle, that's what that stuff is."

"I wonder ..."

We had by now reached the end of the bridle path, and were on the main lane, opposite The Hop Pole Inn.

"Home at last!" she said, happily. "I don't suppose you'd like a drink?"

"Oh, well, I don't ..." Go to pubs. I detested them. Their horrible noise, smoke, smell of alcohol.

"Come on, you only live once! I'll put old Scott here around at the back, and you go on in there. Tell 'em you're my guest."

"And you?"

"I'm Alice."

"All right, Alice."

I entered the establishment, not without a sense of adventure, and, when approached by the barman, ordered a glass of bitter, a drink which I had never tasted and which I supposed I would hate. When it arrived, however, I found that I was thirsty and it delicious, much much tastier than tea at the Pump Room, which was actually the last beverage I'd had, and which had tasted of rusty nails.

I was into my second glass by the time Alice came in, with her hair tied up again in its red bandanna, and a great deal of make-up on her face.

"That's it, make yourself at home!" she plumped down into a plush chair and ordered a double whiskey.

"So tell me about yourself then!"

This is the type of request I normally detest, and answer as shortly as I can without being downright rude. But for some reason, possibly to do with my intake of bitter, I gave Alice a fairly detailed autobiography, telling her about Mother and Daddy, Alasdair, Paddy, the house in Rathmines, my job in a school, and, of course, my night classes.

"Night classes? They sound like fun. Any fine things at it?"

I thought of the night class: fifteen women, ranging in age from eighteen to seventy, and two men, aged sixty-five.

"No. Men don't take night classes much, for some reason."

"Jesus!" she cried, "That amazes me! Why do women take 'em then?"

I did not know.

"Hmm." She pondered this for a minute. "Have another drink!"

"Thanks." The barman deposited a pint of beer on the table in front of me. I was by now tipsy ... tipsier than Jane Austen ever had been, perhaps, or any but the most depraved of her characters. Perhaps ... on the other hand, wine is served at every meal, in the novels.

"So inebriation must have been a possibility, mustn't it?"

"I should think so," nodded Alice. "It usually is."

"Oh, pardon me! I was thinking out loud, about Jane Austen."

"Not her again! Who the hell was this dame anyway?"

"If this were an Austen novel, what would happen now is, Paddy — he's the one I was engaged to — would walk through that door, tell me that word had reached him at Manchester that I was in Bath, that it all had been a terrible misunderstanding, and that he still hoped I would accept his offer of marriage."

"What did I tell you? That woman knew nothing about men, absolutely zilch. Shall I tell you how it's done in reality, speaking as one who's been married more than five times? You go to Manchester, say you've heard Paddy was still there and just happened to be passing through, that it was all a terrible misunderstanding, and shouldn't you go out for dinner and talk it over? That's how it's done in real life, which is not one bit like a Jane Austen novel, my dear. And get your hair streaked before you go."

This piece of crudity might have irritated me, had I not at that moment caught sight of a tall man entering the inn ... the only man to have done so since we'd arrived. The people of Bath are not heavy drinkers. He had red hair, cut quite short, a reddish complexion, a green tweed suit and a conference name label which bore, in large Celtic lettering, the name: "Paddy".

"Paddy!" I cried, "Is it really you?"

"Anita! At last."

He came over to our table and clasped my hand in his for sixty seconds or thereabouts, during which time we gazed into each others' eyes. His were still blue, although a little bloodshot, and there were more wrinkles around them than there had been sixteen years ago, when I'd last seen them, at the twelve bus stop outside Clery's.

"What a coincidence!" I ventured, hoping to hear that it was no such thing.

"It's no coincidence," Paddy retorted, and I breathed a sigh of relief. He proceeded to explain that an old friend of his, Tommy Doyle, was on the excursion with the Rathmines Adult Education Institute, that he'd dropped him a postcard letting him know he would be in Bath, which, incidentally, was where Paddy now lived, teaching in an Adult Education Institute there. When he called on Tommy Doyle at the hotel, Tommy had mentioned that I was of the party, and that he'd seen me popping into The Hop Pole Inn an hour previously. Paddy had lost no time in rushing across the road to join me.

"And who's your pal?" he inquired, when our gazing seemed to be finished.

"That's Alice," I said.

"Alice who?"

I looked at her.

"Oh, they call me Dame Alice around here," she giggled.

"Can I get you a drink, Paddy? What a darling name!" And she winked at him, and ... yes ... wiggled her enormous bottom, as she waddled up to the bar for a double whiskey.

I find it difficult to describe the events which followed this:
they were puzzling for me at the time, and painful in retrospect.
But their outcome was that Alice seduced Paddy, right before
my nose, and, at about midnight, I left them, drinking whiskey
and exchanging confidences, acting as though I did not exist.

I crept out of the pub, vowing never to visit such an
establishment again, and back to my narrow bedroom at the
Limpley Stoke Hotel. My copy of *Sense and Sensibility* was lying
face downward on the pillow. I opened it, and tried to read. But
I couldn't. The Rathmines Adult Education Group was drinking
in the residents' lounge, and the sound of their brash voices,
talking, shouting, and singing — someone, Tommy Doyle, I
think, was giving a very poignant and loud rendering of *The
Town I Loved So Well* — distracted me. I threw the book on my
bed, and paced my room angrily. There was no hope of sleep,
absolutely none. I could not go back to The Hop Pole Inn, never
never never. And to walk alone at night in Limpley Stoke was
inadvisable, unless one were bent on a death of tabloid horror,
which, I realised, after a few moments' consideration, I was not.

What could I do? There was one black dress in my wardrobe,
and one red necklace in my bag: I had bought them the day
before I left Rathmines. Just in case. Quickly I pulled off my
tweeds and slid into the garment, which, I must admit, did
wonders for my figure. I tied the beads around my neck and
rubbed some brownish moisturiser onto my face: the effect of
this was startling: wrinkles and spots vanished before my eyes,
and I had what I had never possessed before: a youthful
complexion. A touch of pencil on the eyes, and then, slowly and
reluctantly, I walked along the corridor. A voice ... Rory's ...
raised in a passionate interpretation of *O Sole Mio!* serenaded me
as I approached the lounge. My heart pounded.

I opened the door and plunged in.

Roz Cowman

Paranoia

Cleaner than the hyena,
I scavenge their lives,
use up the rinds of love,
the gone-sour friendships; I waste
not the unwanted.
Waiting in shadows
until lion leaves his kill,
I beat the vultures to it.
I win.
I snarl over the carcass,
not to warn them off
but from my one
terror ... that this
is no wild life
but a Safari Park
where a warden charts my progress
as I scrounge
from bin to bin.

Dream Of The Red Chamber

Red tides have filled
the estuary; dykes
are down; the land
of the two canals
is gone.

Old hill, if I tread
stepping-stones of black
bungalows back to the first
threshold, the dream
of a red room,

will you accept
my journey as a rite
of passage, and absorb me

as the hare mother absorbs
her foetus children
into her blood

when spring is stillborn,
and late frosts
salt the earth?

Annunciation

All day the sun has poured
its gases into the town;
stone erodes; copper domes
liquify; glare
makes terracotta faces;
plate glass reverts
to silica.

No shade; the late traveller
will find no lapis dusk
to cushion his announcement.
Concrete heaves underfoot;
clouds are significant.

Even the furniture's turned hostile.
In what's left of air, spermatozoa
float like pollen. She would gasp
for breath in the rush
of his descent beside her,
but the atmosphere
vacuums to him,

the frail tympani of her ears
snap like furze-pods,
and with everything still
unsaid between them,
the word is made flesh.

Gerardine Meaney

The Oval Portrait

"A shaft of light pierced the shadow into which her features faded. For an instant her dream-ridden eyes were startled into one swift appraisal of her surroundings. Then she let her hair hang down to one side, deflecting the sun's glare, shattering it into the flecks of gold that were scattered now through the long brown tresses. With the air of one sketching an inner landscape, she raised her pen again and began to draw."

What is he talking about, she wondered, yet she knew this was what she expected.

"This isn't me, it isn't me at all. For one thing, I wear my glasses and screw up my eyes when I paint and you've never seen me draw, it's years since I did."

To prove the point, she threw down the typescript story he had given her and moved towards an easel by the window. As he walked into the room she was staring intently at a half-finished still life, pushing her glasses up to the bridge of her nose with one finger. "It is a story," he wore amusement as if she could not see through that cloak. "You don't paint things as they are, do you? No real fruit bowl ever looked like that."

He was pointing at an oddly angular, disjointed form in the corner of her picture. Something in the shades and textures of the dim colours defied geometry to insist this object was round and full. She was pleased with it, she never intended to paint a real fruit bowl, she had captured something of the rough texture and smooth geometry of the ceramic bowls you see everywhere...

The phrases welled up, but there was no point, it would be emotional and futile. She was too sensitive and he used words so easily. His voice would flow on, appealing, hurt, humorous, all those things. She would understand she had no sense of proportion about her painting, that he had intended no criticism and that artistic temperament was scarcely justified by her ordinary little "pictures".

So she said nothing. He stood beside her, grinning still at the disconcerting bowl. Moving away, she picked up the story again, smiling when he came to sit beside her.

"It isn't me though." So it was unreasonable to feel so uneasy, unreasonable to feel this creeping sense of loss as she read, as though each word stole something from her.

"You wouldn't want to be immortalised with your glasses on, would you? Besides, I thought you'd like to know you present such pretty pictures to my imagination."

She was as uncomfortable to feel his arm round her as with this type-written rival who looked inwards to paint, didn't need decent light, not so much as a table to work on.

The arm slid around her waist and tightened there.

"I can't concentrate with you here. Go on, do some work." She was laughing and kissing him while she pushed him into the other room and closed the door. Then she dropped the story again, walked to the window and peered into the shrill light that was spearing banks of cloud, muted, stippled shadows. Impossible to capture that light, but you could share in its deceptions. You could play with it on shapes that sat solemn, on strait-laced furniture or dejected streets.

"Have you finished it?"

He was eager for her reaction of course. For one second a very clear voice told her he must go. It was shocking, these shafts of cruelty that taunted her, offered her prescriptions so far from her own desires or needs.

"Make me some coffee can't you? How can I read or paint or do anything when you won't leave me alone for two minutes?"

She was sorry, she didn't mean to take it out on him, this unease with herself. She didn't mean to let the cold, hard voice, that wasn't her own voice, be heard.

"I'm sorry," he didn't sound sorry. "The story has offended you, hasn't it? Tell me about it please."

"Tell me, tell me. I need to be alone sometimes, don't I? I'm entitled to a little bad temper now and again."

That wasn't what she wanted to say, it wasn't. He looked angry, no, hurt. She began again,

"I'm sorry, I didn't mean ..."

"Don't be sorry. Admit that the story is bothering you."

Perhaps, she thought, yes it was the story, but more than that.

He said, "I can hardly be sorry they're going to publish it, even for you. I wish you were able to enjoy it when things go well for me, I wish you didn't have to compete all the time, afraid your painting wouldn't be good enough."

That was not his voice, she must remember that, she had hurt his feelings and he didn't mean to say this.

He must have seen something in her face, for something

arrested the crescendo of wishes.

"These things have to be out in the open. You let these barriers build up when you won't discuss things."

That was his voice, gentle and caressing, that was how she described his voice to herself. It continued,

"You know it doesn't matter to me if you're no great artist. I love you for yourself, as they say. Really, you mustn't feel you should keep up with me or whatever it is that makes you panic so."

She panicked now, going to him, clutching the familiar contours of his shoulders and back, or their familiarity, grabbing them to drag herself up from this slow, sucking flow of confusion. He kissed the top of her head.

"I wish it didn't upset you so much to talk about things."

She still could say nothing.

"You have such hair."

She imagined him looking down on it, smiling, and felt she should look up, smile back. She did.

When he had gone out again, she returned to her easel, but she could not paint. The grey light stuttered now and seemed to blur the shape and the texture of things too much, too far.

She gave up trying to peer through that disturbing light. Looking sideways, she saw a few faltering rays of sun filter through her hair. Like that girl in his awful story. "Not awful. Why do I think it's awful? Someone is publishing the thing, after all. Perhaps he is right. I must be jealous."

He knows all about jealousy, of course, the cruel voice broke through again. She could only concur with that.

She remembered the incident last week in one of the pubs they frequented. The inevitable "old friend" turned up. He was with one of those desperately cheerful office parties. He was glad to escape and glad to see her. They had been good friends, she and Owen, when they had both lived in a big, untidy house shared by half a dozen relative strangers.

That was before she met Michael. He had been talking, that night, to someone at the bar. They had ten minutes comfortable recollection before he saw them, frowned, returned, waited for an introduction.

"No, we haven't met." And didn't wish to meet. The other retaliated for the surliness by speaking exclusively to her, until he realised her discomfort. This jealous "insecurity" troubled her, but it thrilled her a little too and she wanted them to be alone, to fight it out, reconcile, whatever. Both men knew her well enough to realise it.

"I'll see you around." Owen's interest was exciting and he

recognised that also. "Soon, I hope?"

The night had not been thrilling. They bickered, raged, she cried.

"Why do you need to bolster up your ego," he asked, "flirting with any fool you meet in a pub?"

Why should she read his story? She would say she felt too close to it to criticise.

There were other stories. She never read them. He asked very tactfully if she would like to talk about her destructive insecurity. She painted less.

He had been very confident that he would win this bursary, but then he had been confident that he would win others, bitter when he did not. Now he was going to Canada for two months and she found herself sobbing, he comforting with the air of a man who found her distress eminently understandable.

"I will miss you just as much, you know. But it's only a couple of months and I wouldn't go if it wasn't important."

In the weeks before he went she felt alternately miserable and euphoric. At times she thought herself so desperately lonely he might have been gone already. Those times were interrupted by moments, created moments, when they felt inseparable, when they anticipated his return, turned two months into a flash, felt it was no more than a moment.

All that feeling. When he was gone she felt nothing. No. She felt nothing for him. For the first week she came home to the flat she had imagined empty and cold and "desolate" and found herself taking a surprising and unprecedented pleasure in it. She ate peculiarly, as she called it, experimenting with whatever odds and ends the corner shop could supply. It occurred to her these experiments turned out well, for she could not remember when she had enjoyed food so much.

After dinner, she wandered around the flat, picking up a novel, peering out into the light, out into swirls of rain that dripped long after from a broken pipe.

She merely dabbled with her paints, losing all sense of form to a delight in colour which quickly bored. Then she returned to peering out the window.

By the second week she was following her gaze, walking for miles, preoccupied with some leaden skyscape. When a pale light succeeded showery darkness she would be fascinated: a shimmer glimpsed on wet greenery would have her wandering until dark.

She was keeping herself occupied, she told herself, though she could not name this occupation. She was bearing it all very well, though sometimes she forgot what she was bearing.

What was wrong? She walked for miles without tiring. She could concentrate on nothing, but her mind was a hive of notions, thoughts, images, impressions. Everything about her was restless too. And light. Lightness was the word for this welling sense of being. There were no burdens on her.

I do not want to be lonely, she sometimes told herself. So she tried on loneliness like an ill-fitting dress. She tried to experience an absence, since no longing for presence was felt. She tried to think of poor Michael, also alone, working, struggling to be heard. The cruel voice allied itself to a mental artist and conjured up a picture of a badly dressed young man sipping wine and talking confidentially to strangers about his projected novel. The cruel voice sounded so like her own, she laughed in complicity for once. Then uneasy, she moved around the room, began daubing, scribbling. The still life had lain to one side for over a year. She toyed with the idea of painting over it, but the oddly tactile attraction of that bowl arrested her.

Hours later, surveying her changes, she remembered. "No real fruit bowl ..." She looked at the patterns of swaying abstractions the still life had become. It would do for a title.

She worked then, she had never worked so hard or so well. She had the benefit of no one's opinion, of course, but sometimes you know these things, she told herself. It was a curiosity that the mundane office procedures which occupied her days and had always seemed so irrelevant and unreal, now acquired life of their own. She had called the job a matter of keeping body and soul together by exiling soul eight hours a day. She had always said that without intelligent company to come home to, she would become a zombie for good. Perhaps that was happening now. For she found herself feeling a kind of nostalgia, a delight in the routine of work and coffee, lunchtime and work as if she returned to such ordinary sights, smells and sensations after a long and unpleasant absence.

She had been coming home from work when she met Owen again, again thinking "how inevitable". Rushing for a train, he proclaimed himself delighted to see her, extracted her telephone number and ran away. It never occurred to her to turn him down when he rang and asked to meet her. Afterwards she could not say whether he was a good listener or had been overwhelmed by her rambling dissertations on everything, herself, her work, new modes, light. But he listened. Then he asked about old things, paintings, friends. While they walked home he said, "It is good to see you like this again."

Drinking coffee on the floor of the flat, he gazed at the sketches and half-begun paintings that had proliferated in the weeks just past. She was still talking about them when they went to bed, laughing at the incongruity of it. All easy, light. For a moment she saw, sideways, the peculiar tactile bowl. Then the real texture of the unfamiliar body beneath her hands absorbed all of her attention.

When he left in the morning, he said she must make up her own mind and she felt the easiness was betrayed. He had come along, now he should stay and focus this euphoria of hers that ebbed with the dragging tide of indecision he left washing from her door. Her anger never subsided, not all day, and in the evening when he rang to say, "Sorry, next Wednesday could they meet?", subsided only to contempt. Next Wednesday.

Well then, no immediate changes. She painted with a fury all that night, thought it bad, threw it there, went to bed, in the morning thought, not bad. That evening and a long walk later, the scars of paint on her canvas seemed to her to mark some sort of a progression.

The letter arrived. Every sentence was of "bustle" "new energy", anecdotes of taxi drivers, "tremendous" things, some writer whose works stood on the shelves here who had proved a "tremendous disappointment" at the Convention. A literary agent had been "very interested". Everyone was "very interested".

She did not finish the letter.

She found her work was changing. Now instead of beginning with some concrete image and transforming it to an abstract form, she moved from form to image. Trees, houses, the curve of a street began to emerge on the canvas under her hand and she realised she was producing a version of the view from her window. Awareness of this frustrated her. She did not care for verisimilitude. Yet the more she tried to abandon that particular view, the more she attempted to lose its specific features, the more persistently those features insinuated themselves from her brush. It would never be a "real street", but it was an image of precisely this street, nonetheless, at this time and in that disconcerting light.

Her office hours speeded by and the nights could not be long enough. On Wednesday morning, Michael's next letter arrived.

You must be lonely, it said. "Why don't you write? Should I write more? Are you angry? You know I'm so busy."

I scarcely find time to eat, she thought, and she wondered

why, why the urgency? Why paint all night after working all day? There was time, plenty of it, she was young. Better write, but after all he will be home in a few weeks ...

She could finish the landscape, if she kept up the pace, and she had a new idea brewing in her now.

She was irritable all day, the office bored her again, she despised it, these people she worked with were beyond belief. When Owen came that night, she had spent an hour glaring into space with a brush in her hand.

"So you decided to turn up, did you?"

The vehemence of the next ten minutes of accusation surprised her no less than him. Then she found herself crying, bursting into tears. He was comforting, put his arms round her, said the soft things people say, but he was distant and, she realised, very, very wary. She was making a fool of herself.

"I am sorry, this is nonsense. I'm a little overtired, that's all. I've been working so hard."

"So I see."

He stared at the canvases. Why couldn't he stop poking around, she thought and noticed her annoyance had not at all abated.

"You'll be a good painter, won't you?"

"How am I supposed to know?"

"Who else ... Look. I like you. I hope all this works out well." His hands indicated the piles of canvases, rough sketches, rags and paints and brushes.

"But?" Why am I bothering to ask, she thought.

"I'm not going to save your life."

What?

"That's being too dramatic, I mean... I'm not sure what I mean."

All this stuttering and stammering, she thought. Then she remembered the letter and found it difficult to think him a complete fool.

"Obviously you want to get out from under this fellow's influence and you want to paint and everything. But I mean, I'm not much use to you. I don't know anything about painting. Except what you told me. More than that, though. I think really, you'd need to be more independent for that kind of thing."

"Are you trying to tell me you don't want commitments?"

She wondered who had taught her to make irrelevant clichés sound so offensive.

"Well, I don't, not this kind."

He looked helpless and confused and she took advantage of it to sound cold and determined when she told him to go, get out, goodbye, no, there was nothing to talk about.

She didn't paint. She reread the letter and found the endearments at the end. "Endearments" was the right word, lots of love on paper. She tried reading novels, tried to sleep. Next day the restlessness continued, a house-bound restlessness that night, for she could not contemplate long walks.

On Friday, another letter from Michael arrived, air-mail. She had not noticed the others were surface. She wondered what prompted such extravagance.

The letter was indignant, it proclaimed itself outraged. She skimmed. She "could not be bothered to write", those days before he left meant nothing, no doubt she was out, around, parties, plenty of attractive women here, yes, he was attracted ... but ... passion ... relationship ... deeply something, attached, committed, over, write, explain. Write, tell me. Tell, tell, tell.

She shook herself. She had behaved badly. It was unfair and selfish, half an hour was all that was needed. Painting could wait that long, painting that might never come to anything. And she was nearly finished this one. When she remembered Owen, she was shocked that she had not remembered him sooner. It was as if she were more guilty about the time spent painting. That lurking voice came out to say that Michael would, in any case, be more jealous of the painting. "Tell, tell, tell me about your insecurity..." She went to the office, but did no work. The painting and the two men. One wanted her to choose. Between what? He was not offering to take the other's place, why should he? Yet she knew she was affronted he did not wish to.

"Get out from under this fellow's influence," as if she lived with a sinister guru of some sort.

So he must be jealous of him. The thought was so satisfactory she began to fantasise about confronting him with it. Then an image of Michael, in this new guise, overpowered her, smothered fantasy. She took out his letter for reassurance, but her sense of dread was choking her, "commitment ... attached ... home soon." Home soon. I have to finish that landscape ...

Her thoughts crystallised, taking on a form that was also an idea.

It was relentless. She tried to ignore it, for she could not argue herself out of this idea of her life that was so bleak, so angry. It was angry, not she. At first. Then it tightened its grip on her. She looked at all her paintings, going back over years. She picked out six or seven, trying to take some initiative . About time she started showing them again. This last one would sell anyway.

Then she took down all of Michael's stories, notes for things he had not written, notebooks of ideas, a plan for the novel. She read each. The stories she read twice. Then she stared a long time out that window. Afterwards she could not recall the first impulse to paint that night. She would have a vague memory of frenzied activity all that weekend, on through the week. She rang the office to say she was ill and she felt as if she were working an infection out of her blood and her mind.

It took two weeks. She had referred to photographs, but they had not helped her. When she saw it was finished, she slept for a very long time. Then she went to the office, where she was accepted only because her face spoke undeniably of recovery from long pain.

The man who framed everything for her cheaply was quite astonished by it. He had a contact who sometimes bought for a small gallery that liked to buy from young artists. She was sorry, she said, this one was promised. There were others, however. What was this contact's name? And he would remember to place this in an oval frame?

She rang Owen to say she was moving, but would ring when she got time. She took the first flat she went to see, packed her bags and her paintings. She looked back only to be sure that the first thing he would see was the framed portrait. It hung on the wall, bare now, opposite the door.

When Michael returned, the painting was not the first thing which engaged his attention. He tripped over his increasingly hysterical letters of the past weeks as soon as he opened the door. Then it struck him.

He found a chair and looked around him. She was gone. Completely. He returned his gaze.

"That isn't me." He needed to say it aloud. He needed to assert himself against it. He looked back at himself, there, in that frame.

The detail was compelling. He never thought she was that good. There was nothing he could argue with, no fault to find. He could not say this, specifically, is wrong, that, precisely, should not be so. Yet the overall effect, that was distortion, terrible, insane, it must be distortion.

"That is not me." And he screamed now.

The bulky package arrived at her office two days later. The features of course were slashed. The frame, however, was immediately recognisable.

Eiléan Ní Chuilleanáin

The Informant

Underneath the photograph
Of the old woman at her kitchen table
With a window beyond (fuschias, a henhouse, the sea)
Are entered: her age, her late husband's occupation
(A gauger), her birthplace, not here,
But in another parish, near the main road.
She is sitting with tea at her elbow
And her own fairy-cakes, baked that morning
For the young man who now listens to the tape
Of her voice changing as she tells
The story, and hears himself asking
Did you ever see it yourself?
                              Once, I saw it.
Can you describe it? The sound
Goes haywire; a tearing, a storm,
And then a silence and the voice again resuming:
       "the locks forced upward, a shift of air
       pulled over the head. The face bent
       and the eyes winced as if craning
       to look in the core of a furnace.
       The man unravelled
       Back to a snag, a dark thread."

And then what happens?
                              The person disappears ––
For a time he remains at hand and speaks
In a child's voice. But he is not seen, and
You must leave food out for him and be careful
Where you throw water after you wash your feet.

And then he is gone?
                       He's gone, after a while.
*You find this more strange than the yearly miracle
Of the loaf turning into a child?*
Well, that's natural, she says.
I often baked the bread for that myself.

171

A Voice

(i)

After coming so far, in response
To a woman's voice, a distant wailing,
Now he can distinguish words:
You may come in,
You are already in.

But the wall is thornbushes, crammed and barbed.
A human skeleton, warped in a dive, is clasped
And grips a flowering briar. His wincing flesh reproves him
As it turns and flows
Backwards like a tide.

(ii)

Knowing it now for a trick of the light
He marches forward, takes account
of true stones and mortared walls,
Downfaces the shimmer
And shakes to hear the voice humming again.

In the bed of the stream
She lies in her bones —
Large bearing hips, and square
Elbows. Around them lodged
Gravegoods of horsehair and an ebony peg.

It persists even here, the ridge in the fingerbone.
"What sort of ornament is this? What sort of mutilation?"
And he hears her voice, a wail of strings.

J'ai Mal à Nos Dents

In memory of Anna Cullinane (Sister Mary Antony)

The Holy Father gave her leave
To return to her father's house
At seventy-eight years of age.

When young in the Franciscan house at Calais
She complained to the dentist, *I have a pain in our teeth*
— Her body dissolving out of her first mother,
Her five sisters aching at home.

Her brother listened to news
Five times in a morning on Radio Eireann
As the Germans entered Calais. Her name lay under the surface
As she worked all day with the Sisters;
They stripped the hospital, they loaded the sick on lorries
And Reverend Mother walked the wards and nourished them
With jugs of wine to hold their strength.
J'étais à moitié saoule. It was done,
They lifted the old sisters on the pig-cart
And the young walked out on the road to Desvres,
The wine still buzzing and the planes over their heads.

Je mangerai les pissenlits par les racines.
A year before she died she lost her French accent;
When she went home in her habit to care for her sister Nora
They handed her back her body,
Its voices and its death.

Mary Dorcey

The Husband

They made love then once more because she was leaving him. Sunlight came through the tall, Georgian window. It shone on the blue walls, the yellow paintwork, warming her pale blonde hair, the white curve of her closed eyelids. He gripped her hands, their fingers interlocked, his feet braced against the wooden footboard. He would have liked to break her from the mould of her body; from its set, delicate lines. His mouth at her shoulder, his eyes were hidden and he was glad to have his back turned on the room; from the bare dressingtable stripped of her belongings and the suitcase open beside the wardrobe.

Outside, other people were going to mass. He heard a bell toll in the distance. A man's voice drifted up: "I'll see you at O'Brien's later", then the slam of a car door and the clatter of a woman's spiked heels hurrying on the pavement. All the usual sounds of Sunday morning rising distinct and separate for the first time in the silence between them. She lay beneath him passive, magnanimous, as though she were granting him a favour, out of pity or gratitude because she had seen that he was not after all going to make it difficult for her at the end. He moved inside her body, conscious only of the sudden escape of his breath, no longer caring what she felt, what motive possessed her. He was tired of thinking, tired of the labour of anticipating her thoughts and concealing his own.

He knew that she was looking past him, over his shoulder towards the window, to the sunlight and noise of the street. He touched a strand of her hair where it lay along the pillow. She did not turn. A tremor passed through his limbs. He felt the sweat grow cold on his back. He rolled off her and lay still, staring at the ceiling where small flakes of whitewash peeled from the moulded corners. The sun had discovered a spider's web above the door, like a square of grey lace its diamond pattern swayed in a draught from the stairs. He wondered how it had survived the winter and why it was he had not noticed it before. Exhaustion seeped through his flesh bringing a sensation of calm. Now that it was over at last he was glad, now that there was nothing more to be done. He had tried everything and failed. He had lived ten years in the space of one -altered himself by the hour to suit her and she had told him it made no difference - that it was useless whatever he did because it had nothing to do with him personally, with individual failing. He could not accept that, could not resign himself to being a mere cog in someone else's political theory. He had done all that he knew to persuade, to understand her. He had been by turns argumentative, patient, sceptical, conciliatory. The night when, finally, she had told him it was over, he had wept in her arms, pleaded with her, vulnerable as any woman, and she had remained indifferent, patronising even; seeing only the male he could not cease to be. They said they wanted emotion, honesty, self-exposure but when they got it, they despised you for it. Once and once only he had allowed the rage in him to break free; let loose the cold fury that had been festering in his gut since the start of it. She had come home late on Lisa's birthday and when she told him where she had been blatantly, flaunting it, he had struck her across the face; harder than he had intended so that a fleck of blood showed on her lip. She had wiped it off with the back of her hand, staring at him, a look of shock and covert satisfaction in her eyes. He knew then in his shame and regret that he had given her the excuse she had been waiting for.

He looked at her now, at the hard pale arch of her cheekbone. He waited for her to say something but she kept silent and he could not let himself speak the only words that were in his mind. She would see them as weakness. Instead, he heard himself say her name, "Martina", not wanting to, but finding it form on his lips from force of habit; a sound, a collection of syllables that had once held absolute meaning and now meant nothing or too much, composed as it was of so many conflicting memories.

She reached a hand past his face to the breakfast cup that stood on the bedside table. A dark, puckered skin had formed on the coffee's surface but she drank it anyway. "What?" she said without looking at him. He felt that she was preparing her next move, searching for a phrase or gesture that would carry her painlessly out of his bed and from their flat. But when she did speak again there was no attempt at prevarication or tact. "I need to shower," she said bluntly, "can you let me out?" She swung her legs over the side of the bed, pushing back the patterned sheet, and stood up. He watched her walk across the room away from him. A small mark like a circle of chalk dust gleamed on the muscle of her thigh - his seed dried on her skin. The scent and taste of him would be all through her. She would wash meticulously every inch of her body to remove it. He heard her close the bathroom door behind her and a moment later the hiss and splatter of water breaking on the shower curtain. Only a few weeks ago she would have run a bath for them both and he would have carried Lisa in to sit between their knees. Yesterday afternoon he had brought Lisa over to her mother's house. Martina had said she thought it was best if Lisa stayed there for a couple of weeks until they could come to some arrangement. Some arrangement! For Lisa! He knew then how crazed she was. Of course, it was an act - a pretence of consideration and fairmindedness, wanting it to appear that she might even debate the merits of leaving their daughter with him. But he knew what she planned, all too well.

He had a vision of himself calling over to Leinster Road on a Saturday afternoon, standing on the front step ringing the bell. Martina would come to the door and hold it open staring at him blankly as if here were a stranger, while Lisa ran to greet him. Would Helen be there too with that smug, tight, little smile on her mouth? Would they bring him in to the kitchen and make tea and small talk while Lisa got ready, or would they have found some excuse to have her out for the day? He knew every possible permutation, he had seen them all a dozen times on television and seventies' movies but he never thought he might be expected to live out these banalities himself. His snort of laughter startled him. He could not remember when he had last laughed aloud. But who would not at the idea that the mother of his child could imagine that this cozy Hollywood scenario might become reality? When she had first mentioned it, dropping it casually as a vague suggestion, he had forced himself to hold back the derision that rose to his tongue. He would say nothing. Why should he? Let her learn the hard way. They would all say it for him soon enough - his parents, her mother. The instant they discovered the truth, who and what she had left him for, they would snatch Lisa from her as ruthlessly as they would from quicksand. They would not be shackled by any qualms of conscience. They would have none of his need to show fine feeling. It was extraordinary that she did not seem to realise this herself, unthinkable that she might not allow it to influence her.

She came back into the room, her legs bare beneath a shaggy red sweater. The sweater he had bought her for christmas. Her nipples protruded like two small stones from under the loose wool. She opened the wardrobe and took out a pair of blue jeans and a grey corduroy skirt. He saw that she was on the point of asking him which he preferred. She stood in the unconsciously childish pose she assumed whenever she had a decision to make, however trivial, her feet apart, her head tilted to one side. He lay on his back watching her, his hands interlaced between the pillow and his head. He could feel the blood pulsing behind his ears but he kept his face impassive. She was studying her image in the mirror, eyes wide with anxious vanity. At last she dropped the jeans into the open case and began to pull on the skirt. Why - was that what Helen would have chosen? What kind of look did she go for? Elegant, sexy, casual? But then, they were not into looks - oh no, it was all on a higher, spiritual plane. Or was it? What did she admire in her anyway? Was it the same qualities as he did or something quite different, something hidden from him? Was she turned on by some reflection of herself or by some opposite trait, something lacking in her own character? He could not begin to guess. He knew so little about this woman Martina was abandoning him for. He had left it too late to pay her any real attention. He had been struck by her the first night, he had to admit, meeting her in O'Brien's after that conference. He liked her body; the long legs and broad shoulders and something attractive in the sultry line of her mouth. A woman he might have wanted himself in other circumstances. If he had not been told immediately that she was a lesbian. Not that he would have guessed it - at least not at first glance. She was too good-looking for that. But it did not take long to see the coldness in her, the chip on her shoulder; the arrogant, belligerent way she stood at the bar and asked him what he wanted to drink. But then she had every reason for disdain, had she not? She must have known already that his wife was in love with her. It had taken him a year to reach the same conclusion.

She sat on the bed to put on her stockings, one leg crossed over the other. He heard her breathing - quick little breaths through her mouth. She was nervous then. He stared at the round bone of her ankle as she drew the red mesh over it. He followed her hands as they moved up the length of her calf. Her body was so intimately known to him he felt he might have cast the flesh on her bones with his own fingers. He saw the stretch marks above her hip. She had lost weight this winter. She looked well but he preferred her as she used to be - voluptuous, the plump roundness of her belly and arms. He thought of all the days and nights of pleasure that they had had together. She certainly could not complain that he had not appreciated her. He would always be grateful for what he had discovered with her. He would forget none of it. But would she? Oh no. She pretended to have forgotten already. She talked now as though she had been playing an elaborate game all these years going through ritual actions to please him. When he refused to let her away with that kind of nonsense, the deliberate erasure of their past and forced her to acknowledge the depth of passion there had been between them, she said yes, she did not deny that they had had good times in bed but it had very little to with him. He had laughed in her face. And who was it to do with then? Who else could take credit for it? She did not dare to answer but even as he asked the question he knew the sort of thing she would come out with. One of Helen's profundities - that straight women use men as instruments, that they make love to themselves through a man's eyes, stimulate themselves with his desire and flattery but that it is their own sensuality they get off on. He knew every version of their theories by now.

"Would you like some more coffee?" she asked him when she had finished dressing. She was never so hurried that she could go without coffee. He shook his head and she walked out of the room pulling a leather belt through the loops of her skirt. He listened to her light footstep on the stairs. After a moment he heard her lift the mugs from their hooks on the wall. He heard her fill the percolator with water, place it on the gas stove and after a while its rising heart beat as the coffee bubbled through the metal filter. He hung on to each sound, rooting himself in the routine of it, wanting to hide in the pictures they evoked. So long as he could hear her moving about in the kitchen below him, busy with all her familiar actions, it seemed that nothing much could be wrong.

Not that he believed that she would really go through with it. Not all the way. Once it dawned on her finally that indulging this whim would mean giving up Lisa she would have to come to her senses. Yes, she would be back soon enough with her tail between her legs. He had only to wait. But he would not let her see that he knew this. It would only put her back up - bring out all her woman's pride and obstinacy. He must tread carefully. Follow silently along this crazy pavement she had laid, step by step, until she reached the precipice. And when she was forced back, he would be there, waiting.

If only he had been more cautious from the beginning. If only he had taken it seriously, recognised the danger in time, it would never have reached this stage. But how could he have? How could any normal man have seen it as any more than a joke? He had felt no jealousy at all at the start. She had known it and been incensed. She had accused him of typical male complacency. She had expected scenes, that was evident, wanted them, had tried to goad him into them. But for weeks he had refused to react with anything more threatening than good humoured sarcasm. He remembered the night she first confessed that Helen and she had become lovers; the anxious, guilty face, expecting god knows what extremes of wrath, and yet underneath it there had been a look of quiet triumphalism. He had had to keep himself from laughing. He was taken by surprise, undoubtedly, though he should not have been with the way they had been going on -never out of each other's company, the all night talks and the heroine worship. But frankly he would not have thought Martina was up to it. Oh, she might flirt with the idea of turning on a woman but to commit herself was another thing. She was too fundamentally healthy, and too fond of the admiration of men. Besides, knowing how passionate she was, he could not believe she would settle for the caresses of a woman.

Gradually his amusement had given way to curiosity, a pleasurable stirring of erotic interest. Two women in bed together after all - there was something undeniably exciting in the idea. He had tried to get her to share it with him, to make it something they could both enjoy but out of embarrassment, or some misplaced sense of loyalty she had refused. He said to tease her, to draw her out a little, that he would not have picked Helen for the whip and jackboots type. What did he mean by that, she had demanded menacingly. And when he explained that as, obviously, she herself could not be cast as the butch, Helen was the only remaining candidate, she had flown at him, castigating his prejudice and condescension. Clearly it was not a topic amenable to humour. She told him that all that role playing was a creation of men's fantasies. Dominance and submission were models women had consigned to the rubbish heap. It was all equality and mutual respect in this brave new world. So where did the excitement, the romance come in, he wanted to ask. If they had dispensed with all the traditional props, what was left? But he knew better than to say anything. They were so stiff with analysis and theory, the lot of them, it was impossible to get a straightforward answer. Sometimes he had even wondered if they were really lesbians at all. Apart from the fact that they looked perfectly normal there seemed something overdone about it. It seemed like a public posture, an attitude struck to provoke men - out of spite or envy. Certainly they flaunted the whole business unnecessarily, getting into fights in the street or in pubs, because they insisted on their right to self-expression and that the rest of the world should adapt to them. He had even seen one of them at a conference sporting a badge on her lapel that read: "How dare you presume I'm heterosexual." Why on earth should anyone presume otherwise unless she was proud of resembling a male impersonator?

And so every time he had attempted to discuss it rationally they had ended by quarrelling. She condemned him of every macho fault in the book and sulked for hours but afterwards they made it all up in bed. As long as she responded in the old manner, so he knew he had not much to worry about. He had even fancied that it might improve their sex life - add a touch of the unknown. He had watched closely to see if any new needs or tastes might creep into her lovemaking.

It was not until the night she had come home in tears that he was forced to rethink his position.

She had arrived in, half-drunk, at midnight after one of their interminable meetings and raced straight up to bed without so much as greeting him or going in to kiss Lisa goodnight. He had followed her up and when he tried to get in beside her to comfort her she had become hysterical, screamed at him to leave her alone, to keep his hands away from her. It was hours before he managed to calm her down and get the whole story out of her. It seemed that Helen had told her that evening in the pub that she wanted to end the relationship. He was astonished. He had always taken it for granted that Martina would be the first to tire. He was even insulted on her behalf. He soothed and placated her stroking her hair and murmuring soft words the way he would with Lisa. He told her not to be a fool, that she was far too beautiful to be cast aside by Helen, that she must be the best thing that had ever happened to her. She was sobbing uncontrollably but she stopped long enough to abuse him when he said that. At last she had fallen asleep in his arms but for the first time he had stayed awake after her. He had to admit that her hysteria had got to him. He could see then it had become some kind of obsession. Up to that he had imagined it was basically a schoolgirl crush, the sort of thing most girls worked out in their teens. But women were so sentimental. He remembered a student of his saying years ago that men had friendships and women had affairs. He knew exactly what he meant. You had only to watch them, perfectly average housewives sitting in cafes or restaurants together, gazing into each other's eyes in a way that would have embarrassed the most besotted man, the confiding tones they used, the smiles of flattery and sympathy flitting between them, the intimate gestures, touching the other's hand, the little pats and caresses, exasperating waiters while they fought over the right to treat one another.

He had imagined that lesbian lovemaking would have some of this piquant quality. He saw it as gently caressive - tender and solicitous. He began to have fantasies about Martina and Helen together. He allowed himself delicious images of their tentative, childish sensuality. When he and Martina were fucking he had often fantasised that Helen was there too, both women exciting each other and then turning to him at the ultimate moment, competing for him. He had thought it was just a matter of time before something like it came about. It had not once occurred to him, in all that while, that they would continue to exclude him; to cut him out mentally and physically, to insist on their self-sufficiency and absorption. Not even that night lying sleepless beside her while she snored, as she always did after too many pints. It did not register with him finally until the afternoon he came home unexpectedly from work and heard them together.

There was no illusion after that, no innocence or humour. He knew it for what it was. Weeks passed before he could rid his mind of the horror of it; it haunted his sleep and fuelled his days with a seething, putrid anger. He saw that he had been seduced, mocked, cheated, systematically, coldbloodedly by assumptions she had worked carefully to foster; defrauded and betrayed. He had stood at the bottom of the stairs - his stairs - in his own house and listened to them. He could hear it from the hall. He listened transfixed, a heaving in his stomach, until the din from the room above rose to a wail. He had covered his ears. Tender and solicitous had he said? More like cats in heat! As he went out of the house slamming the door after him he thought he heard them laughing. Bitches - bloody, fucking bitches! He had made it as far as the pub and ordered whiskey. He sat drinking it - glass after glass, grasping the bowl so hard he might have snapped it in two. He was astounded by the force of rage unleashed in him. He would have liked to put his hands around her bare throat and squeeze it until he had wrung that noise out of it.

Somehow he had managed to get a grip of himself. He had had enough sense to drink himself stupid - too stupid to do anything about it that night. He had slept on the floor in the sittingroom and when he woke at noon she had already left for the day. He was glad. He was not going to humiliate himself by fighting for her over a woman. He was still convinced that it was a temporary delirium; an infection that, left to run its course, would sweat itself out. He had only to wait, to play it cool, to think and to watch until the fever broke.

She came back into the room carrying two mugs of coffee. She set one down beside him, giving a little nervous smile. She had forgotten he had said he did not want any. "Are you getting up?" she asked, as she took her dressing gown from the back of the door, "there's some bread in the oven - will you remember to take it out?"

Jesus! How typical of her - to bake bread the morning she was leaving. The dough had been left as usual, of course, to rise overnight and she could not bring herself to waste it. Typical of her sublime insensitivity! He had always been baffled by this trait in her - this attention, in no matter what crisis, to the everyday details of life and this compulsion to make little gestures of practical concern. Was it another trick of hers to forestall criticism? Or did she really have some power to rise above her own and other people's emotion? But most likely it was just straightforward, old-fashioned guilt.

"Fuck the bread," he said and instantly regretted it. She would be in all the more hurry now to leave. She went to the wardrobe and began to lift down her clothes, laying them in the suitcase. He watched her hands as they expertly folded blouses, jersies, jeans, studying every movement so that he would be able to recapture it precisely when she was gone. It was impossible to believe that he would not be able to watch her like this the next day and the day after. That was what hurt the most. The thought that he would lose the sight of her - just that. That he would no longer look on while she dressed or undressed, prepared a meal, read a book or played with Lisa. Every movement of her body familiar to him, so graceful, so completely feminine. He felt that if he could be allowed to watch her through glass, without speaking, like a child gazing through a shop window, he could have been content. He would not dare express it, needless to say. She would have sneered at him. Objectification, she would call it.

"A woman's body is all that ever matters to any one of you, isn't it?" And he would not argue because the thing he really prized would be even less flattering to her - her vulnerability, her need to confide, to ask his advice in every small moment of self-doubt, to share all her secret fears. God how they had talked! Hours of it. At least she could never claim that he had not listened. And in the end he had learned to need it almost as much as she did. To chat in the inconsequential way she had; curled together in bed, sitting over a glass of wine till the small hours - drawing out all the trivia of personal existence: the dark, hidden things that bonded you forever to the one person who would hear them from you. Was that a ploy too? A conscious one? Or merely female instinct to tie him to her by a gradual process of self-exposure so that he could not disentangle himself, even now, when he had to, because there was no longer any private place left in him, nowhere to hide from her glance, nowhere that she could not seek out and name the hurt in him.

It was this knowledge that had let her see the pain in him, when she woke this morning, behind his closed eyes, that had caused her to make love with him. Another of those little generous acts: handing over her body as you would a towel to someone bleeding. And he had accepted it, idiot that he was - little fawning lap-dog that she had made of him.

She was sitting at the dressing table brushing her hair with slow, attentive strokes, drawing the brush each time from the crown of her head to the tips of her hair where it lay along her shoulder. Was she deliberately making no show of haste, pretending to be doing everything as normal? It seemed to him there must be something he could say; something an outsider would think of immediately. He searched his mind but nothing came to him but the one question that had persisted in him for days: 'Why are you doing this? I don't understand why you're doing this?' She opened a bottle of cologne and dabbed it lightly on her wrists and neck. She always took particular care preparing herself to meet Helen. Helen, who herself wore some heavy French scent that clung to everything she touched, that was carried home in Martina's hair and clothing after every one of their sessions. But that was perfectly acceptable and politically correct. Adorning themselves for each other — make-up, perfume, eyebrow plucking, exchanging clothes — all these feminine tricks took on new meaning because neither of them was a man. Helen did not need to flatter, she did not need to patronise or idolise, she did not need to conquer or submit and her desire would never be exploitative because she was a woman dealing with a woman!

Neither of them had institutionalised power behind them. This was the logic he had been taught all that winter. They told one another these fairy stories sitting round at their meetings. Everything that had ever gone wrong for any one of them, once discussed in their consciousness raising groups could be chalked up as a consequence of male domination. And while they sat about indoctrinating each other with this schoolgirl pap, sounding off on radio and television, composing joint letters to the press, he had stayed at home three nights a week to mind Lisa, clean the house, cook meals, and read his way through the bundles of books she brought home - sentimental novels and half-baked political theses that she had insisted he must look at if he was to claim any understanding at all. And at the finish of it, when he had exhausted himself to satisfy her caprices, she said that he had lost his spontaneity, that their relationship had become stilted, sterile and self-conscious. With Helen, needless to say, all was otherwise - effortless and instinctive. God, he could not wait for their little idyll to meet the adult world; the world of electricity bills, dirty dishes and childminding, and see how far their new roles got them. But he had one pleasure in store before then, a consolation prize he had been saving himself. As soon as she was safely out of the house, he would make a bonfire of them - burn every one - every goddamn book with the word woman on its cover!

She fastened the brown leather suitcase, leaving open the lock on the right hand that had broken the summer two years ago when they had come back from Morocco laden down with blankets and caftans. She carried it across the room, trying to lift it clear of the floor, but it was too heavy for her and dragged along the boards. She went out the door and he heard it knocking on each step as she walked down the stairs. He listened. She was doing something in the kitchen but he could not tell what. There followed a protracted silence. It hit him suddenly that she might try to get out of the flat, leave him and go without saying anything at all. He jumped out of bed, grabbed his trousers from the chair and pulled them on, his fingers so clumsy with haste he caught his hair in the zip. Fuck her! When he rooted under the bed for his shoes she heard and called up: "Don't bother getting dressed, I'll take the bus." She did not think he was going to get the car out and drive her over there, surely? He took a shirt from the floor and pulled it on over his head as he took the stairs to the kitchen two at a time. She was standing by the stove holding a cup of coffee. This endless coffee drinking of hers; cups all over the house, little white rings marked on every stick of furniture. At least he would not have that to put up with any longer.

"There's some in the pot if you want it," she said. He could see the percolator was almost full, the smell of it would be all over the flat now, and the smell of the bloody bread in the oven, for hours after she was gone.

"Didn't you make any tea?"

"No," she said and gave one of her sidelong, maddening looks of apology as though it was some major oversight, "but there's water in the kettle."

"Thanks," he said, "I won't bother."

He was leaning his buttocks against the table, his feet planted wide apart, his hands in his pockets. He looked relaxed and in control at least. He was good at that - years of being on stage before a class of students. He wondered if Helen would come to meet her at the bus stop or was she going to have to lug the suitcase alone all the way up Leinster Road? He wondered how they would greet each other. With triumph or nervousness?

Might there be a sense of anti-climax about it now that she had finally committed herself after so much stalling? Would she tell Helen that she had made love with him before leaving? Would she be ashamed of it and say nothing? But probably Helen would take it for granted as an insignificant gesture to male pride, the necessary price of freedom. And suddenly he wished that he had not been so restrained with her; so much the considerate, respectful friend she had trained him to be. He wished that he had taken his last opportunity and used her body as any other man would have - driven the pleasure out of it until she had screamed as he had heard her that day, in his bed, with her woman lover. He should have forced her to remember him as something more than the tiresome child she thought she had to pacify.

She went to the sink and began to rinse the breakfast things under the tap.

"Leave them," he said "I'll do them," the words coming out of him too quickly. He was losing his cool. She put the cup down and dried her hands on the tea towel. He struggled to think of something to say. He would have to find something. His mind seethed with ridiculous nervous comments. He tried to pick out a phrase that would sound normal and yet succeed in gaining her attention; in arresting this current of meaningless actions that was sweeping between them. And surely there must be something she wanted to say to him? She was not going to walk out and leave him as if she was off to the pictures? She took her raincoat from the bannister and put it on but did not fasten it. The belt trailed to one side. She lifted up the suitcase and carried it into the hallway. He followed her. When she opened the door he saw that it was raining. A gust of wind caught her hair, blowing it into her eyes. He wanted to say "fasten your coat - you're going to get cold" but he did not and he heard himself ask instead, "Where can I ring you?" He had not intended that, he knew the answer. He had the phone number by heart.

She held open the door with one hand and set down the case. She stared down at his shoes and then past him the length of the hallway. Two days ago he had started to sand and stain the floorboards. She looked as if she was estimating how much work remained to be done.

"Don't ring this weekend. We're going away for a while."

He felt a flash of white heat pass in front of his brain and a popping sound like a light bulb exploding. He felt dizzy and his eyes for a moment seemed to cloud over. Then he realised what had happened. A flood of blind terror had swept through him, unmanning him, because she had said something totally unexpected - something he had not planned for. He repeated the words carefully hoping she would deny them, make sense of them.

"You're going away for a while?"

"Yes."

"Where to, for god's sake?" he almost shrieked.

"Down the country for a bit - to friends."

He stared at her blankly, his lips trembling and then the words came out that he had been holding back all morning:

"For how long? When will you be back?"

He could have asked it at anytime, he had been on the verge of it a dozen times and had managed to repress it because he had to keep to his resolve not to let her see that he knew what all this was about - a drama, a show of defiance and autonomy. He could not let her guess that he knew full well she would be back. Somewhere in her heart she must recognise that no one would ever care for her as much as he did. No one could appreciate her more or make more allowances for her. She could not throw away ten years of his life for this - to score a political point - for a theory - for a woman! But he had not said it, all morning. It was too ridiculous - it dignified the thing even to mention it. And now she had tricked him into it, cheated him.

"When will you be back?" he had asked.

"I'll be away for a week, I suppose. You can ring the flat on Monday."

The rain was blowing into her face, her lips were white. She leaned forward. He felt her hand on his sleeve. He felt the pressure of her ring through the cloth of his shirt. She kissed him on the forehead. Her lips were soft, her breath warm on his skin. He hated her then. He hated her body - her woman's flesh that was still caressive and yielding when the heart inside it was shut like a trap against him.

"Goodbye," she said. She lifted the case and closed the door after her.

He went back into the kitchen. But not to the window. He did not want to see her walking down the road. He did not want to see her legs in their scarlet stockings, and the raincoat blown back from her skirt. He did not want to see her dragging the stupid case, to see it banging against her knees as she carried it along the street. So he stood in the kitchen that smelled of coffee and bread baking. He stood over the warmth of the stove, his head lowered, his hands clenched in his pockets, his eyes shut.

She would be back anyhow - in a week's time. She had admitted that now. "In a week," she had said, "ring me on Monday." He would not think about it until then. He would not let himself react to any more of these theatrics. It was absurd the whole business. She had gone to the country, she was visiting friends. He would not worry about her. He would not think about her at all, until she came back.

Áine Ní Ghlinn

Ospidéal

Diúlann na cuirtíní an geimhreadh.
Séideann soprán na gaoithe
go macallach tríothu.

Borrann brollach mór cuirtíneach
chuig an nóta is airde, critheann
agus traoitheann le tromosnaíl anála.

Ionsaíonn banaltra an scáineadh
a beola amhail beart bráillín
iad fillte iarnáilte.

Dúnann sí amach an geimhreadh.
I scornach na fuinneoige
éagann glothar.

Hospital

The curtains suck the winter./The wind-soprano sings/and
echoes through.

A breast of curtain swells/to the highest note, quivers/and falls
with a deep sigh.

A nurse divides the cleavage/her lips are folded sheets/ironed
flat.

She shuts the winter out./In the window's throat/a rattle dies.

(Trans. Máirín Ní Dhonnchadha)

Gairdín Pharthais

Tráth dá raibh
fadó
bhí gairdín
agus beirt 'na luí
— beirt a bhí
'na macasamhail
dá chéile
— beirt nár thuig
aon ní
ach go raibh
gairdín ann
is Garraíodóir
á fhaire ...

Bhíodar ansan 'na luí faoi chrann
go dtí go bhfaca duine acu
úll ar crochadh os a chionn
is dúirt: "Dá mblaisfimis den úll
bheimis ansan chomh feasach
le máistir an ghairdín!"

Chlaon an tarna fear a cheann
ach shín an chéad fhear lámh amach
is thóg ...
is bhlais ...

Nuair a chonaic a chomrádaí
an borradh feasa
i súile an fhir eile
ghéill dá éad, dá ocras
agus d'itheadar araon
is le gach greim
bhuail tonn mhór feasa iad
is le gach greim
mhéadaigh a ndúil
is cé go rabhadar
lán go béal
ba mhór a n-ocras ...
Faoi dheireadh chodlaíodar ...

Dhúisigh siad
le coiscéim an gharraíodóra
a chonaic a bpeaca 'na súile
cé go raibh an crann arís faoi bhláth
is thóg sé siúd dhá úll ón gcrann
is dúirt leis an té a bhlais ar dtús
"Bíodh an dá úll seo agatsa
á gcaitheamh agat gar dod chroí
go deo na ndeor
i gcuimhne ar do pheaca.
Tabharfar ortsa bean
is bíodh dúil shíoraí
ag do chomrádaí
in eolas na n-úll!"

D'oscail sé geataí Pharthais
is dhíbir sé amach san uaigneas iad.
D'imigh an bhean léi
a dá úll ag luascadh roimpi
an fear á leanúint
é ag bárcadh allais.

The Garden of Paradise

Long ago/there was a garden/with two lying there/— two who
were/the image/of each other/— neither understanding/
anything/but that there was/a garden/and a gardener/
watching over it ...

There they lay under a tree/until one saw an apple/right above
his head/and said: "Were we to taste this apple/we would be as
wise/as the master of the garden!"

The other turned his head away/but the first reached out his
hand and took .../and tasted ...

When his companion saw/the knowledge growing/in the
other's eyes/he gave in to envy, to hunger/and together they
ate./With every bite/a great wave of knowledge hit them/and
with each bite/their longing grew/and although they ate/their
fill/they hungered all the more ...

They awoke to hear/the gardener's footstep/and in their eyes he saw their sin/though the tree was again in fruit/and he took two apples from the tree/and said to him who tasted first/'"Take these two apples/and wear them near your heart/for evermore/remembering your sin./You will be known as woman/and let your companion forever crave/the knowledge of your fruit!"

He opened the gates of Paradise/and cast them out into the wilderness./The woman set off/her apples swinging before her,/the man following behind,/sweating profusely.

(Trans. Máirín Ní Dhonnchadha).

Coilltiú

Nuair a d'éirigh sí an mhaidin úd
ba chrann í is ní nárbh ionadh.

Leis na blianta bhí na fréamhacha á hionsaí
nó gur deineadh géaga criogánacha dá lámha.

Iad ag lúbarnaíl aníos nó gur ghlac siad
seilbh faoi dheireadh ina héadan.

Is an mhaidin úd níor éalaigh as a béal
ach tollghíoscán.

Wooden

When she awoke that morning/she had turned to tree and it
was no surprise.

Beset by roots for many years/until her hands became gnarled
branches.

They twisted up and up until at last/they bedded in her
forehead.

And that morning there was no sound from her mouth/only a
hollow creak.

(Trans. Máirín Ní Dhonnchadha)

Anne Le Marquand Hartigan

In That Garden of Paradise

In that garden once she took down the Apple
Casually because she wanted to know, and then
There was all that fuss, Adam going
Bananas saying that she'd tipped the apple cart
And God.
Oh God was a pain getting all huffed up about
His tree and the serpent splitting its sides
Under the bushes laughing.
To save face after all night discussions behind
Closed gates they decided on a lockout. Adam
Raging that he was implicated because of the odd
Bite he took in case She knew more than he did.

She did of course and now she knew it made no
Difference which side of the gates of paradise
They were; until God took a good look at himself
And saw his own womb, his own breast, and not only
His staff of righteousness.

Cysterns

Mother. Step up from under that sod,
push aside my father, that dirty earth
shove it off. I need to know what
you are doing there dead.

What a waste of time. Your thin strong arms
capable of breaking grass roots;
splitting the daisy sods apart apart
lying there; as if in a double bed
pretending for the children
all is well with your marriage. See:
the tombstone is loose, it heels over,
that's a good sign, you're rebelling at last.

Your cheek to my cheek,
our tears spring from the same cystern.
Wipe them off! What are you doing there?
Neat; in the Oppressor's country?

Origins. Danceheat

Yes:
You are a man with magic on you.
You come from stones I have no knowledge of.
You must *talk talk talk*
To me   *words of body*
             words of flesh.
We must eat each other.
Without us mountains may die;
Stones will hatch eggs of serpents,
        the black eye
        shut.
No:
Your feet will twist the air,
My words explode the wind.

Una Woods

Edge Of Lull

Now. Can we talk?

This dull quiet. From where this dull quiet recognised its birth. Shadow birth dull quiet on that road. An on. On for all dull quiet. For example a closed door. Enough for all dull quiet a closed door. Or nothing happening. All dull quiet nothing happening. Another. Yes it remembers. The dull quiet recognises a friend in an empty chapel. Smell of an old woman's clothes. Yes. Enough for dull quiet the smell in the shadow. And. Lisping lips a kind of silent echo. How dull quiet. And the presence. The end of all dull quiet the presence in the tabernacle. Or beginning. Beginning of what dull quiet knew. In what quiet what dull. Or vice versa. How dull quiet the lifting high the chalice. The shaking the incense. How dull the quiet the bowed heads. Quiet the dull the lone Latin voice. Its slow drone.

A Sunday evening. The duller the quieter. How duller quieter can you get? A Sunday evening in Spring coming light on the road. Oh yes. Creeping up that road. Whichever filled the road. Emptied the road. Creeping down that shadow slant. Silent houses deserted factory pale light its flimsy joy of Spring. Just flimsy the dull of that evening light.

And you?

How flimsy veiled through the lace curtains. Ah. flimsy quiet veil of light its slow fall. Flicker on the bare road. Bare paving stones their odd click heels. Sudden echo. Fall back the silence, the weak sink of early summer. On the quiet road recognised dull and almost flimsy joy. Some kind of substance in between. What? Some kind of shadow border of light. Waver of just. Then behind the voices. Recognised the voices.

Voices? Whose voices?

Ssh. Recognise the voices their pull back from that waver of border. Owned themselves those voices. Owned themselves lull of voices in the parlour. Own their lull.

Why do you never say "I" or "my"?

What to say?

Look in the mirror. What do you see?

Some reflection.

Who do you see?

Some reflection.

It is you.

(Staring) Does it know?

It knows.

Or doesn't know. Even that. Even that for definite. To not know for definite. How soothing a thought. To sleep with that for sure. End the uncertainty. It doesn't know it is you. How final.

Look we'll leave it at that for the moment.

Leave it? For the moment? Oh, you are going. Fine.

We do not appear to be getting anywhere. Just now.

A place to get through there to get. Through the attic window big wooden chair drawn over. Rooftops of city streets. Very beyond the light touched the green hills. The hills from the attic where no light. Yet only from the attic. Touched light down on the far green hills from the attic.

Right. I'll see you tomorrow then. We'll talk some more. Goodnight.

Goodnight.

Gone. Now my pad. Pen.

Gone. Her very goneness leaves some space. For all the space you know. To fill the space of her goneness with all the space you know. Again that filled space empties itself. Its very clutter. You recall a clutter of you. But why tell her? Why reveal so much as that clutter of you in your now remembered space. Bright full light down the Friday afternoon risen all hopes in its instant pay day for example. Fragile hope of you in his volatile good humour. That ephemeral singing into the mirror. What fragile share of her hope? Fragile share of her fragile hope. Broken that would live broken as lived. Lived as broken as your role of no role. Recognise some role of no role in the cluttered light. Slanted shadow. Just at its break. You recognise the break though not yourself. Some place you came to occupy. Along that broken line.

As true to yourself as you can get, she said. As true to yourself. How simple a task. How impossible a simple task. The self you do not recognise? Or a different standard. Another standard altogether. Some edge of the broken line you came to nearly occupy. Yes. That. Surely that will do.

As said the white cottage. Twisted up a lane past Howe's. Door opened a whiff of such sea air. Expanse of what lay down before you. Sea sky racing and small whins blowing hard. Small dry whins. Light pale.

Pale everywhere. So recognised the pale. Her face in the doorway eyes filled with such light sea expanse. He maybe behind. Somehow the shaving soap. Somehow the singing. A fresh complexion to descend to the village. Your brothers on the stony front.

Donned his hat and set out down the mountain path. Glimpse the don of hat the figure smaller down the curve of path. Glimpse still there where on the stony front. Crunch of grey stones. All glimpse beneath that racing sky outside the white cottage. And on down through the whins towards the village. A cold air everywhere. Just. Just cold of pale air you recognise. Flap of it about the cottage door. Enough for glimpse the flap of pale air about the cottage door.

Now. Steady trotting sound. Trot. Clop, clop of hooves hear steady on that stretch of road. The trotting trotting suddenly enough into the silence. And on. Smaller on the road the quiet on and on of hooves. Or high from the narrow seat though joggled to the left below sun glint on a piece of water. Bright glint in the width. And as though beyond. The open sea its squint of light laid bare. Moving flat to thin horizon. Thin dab of line between. Thin for dab the fade of meeting place. Never met. Joggled on the narrow seat under the tartan rug. They can only see the mountain, your brother said nudging you and laughed. The trap shook precariously.

Look I told you not to touch me. You held grimly to the rug and stared ahead not to encourage him. Your younger brother piping little nonsensical questions on the other side. Between mother and grandmother.

Pinpoint of split second dim voices. Shadow fall on their side. The close rise of the mountain. Back to your back. Out of your sight. In all of it. Its narrow squint the wide flat light. The dark slope. Low voices. Owned their voices. Their split second lull. Grandmother. Mother. Back to your back on the Carlingford road.

Recognise edge of lull all then.

Celebration

Its own swept smudge of colour enough for birth. Its always return the stroke of sunlit colour. Call it birth. Its worthy part the sudden light. Though uncertain worthy of recognition. Surely. (If ever word ill dreamed-up.) Better enough. Enough for recognition of life the smudge of wavering light. There.

You recognised time and again. Its repeat of when you first opened your eyes. In a cold bedroom your mother celebrated your birth. Alone. In a freezing March where outside the snow thickened on the pavement. Some only glare of white flickering outside your wrapped blanket. Enough. Else some lonely state as yet unresolved. Just started out already in its no resolution. Or. Split second of their merged recognition such life out of that. Its only celebration.

Yet somehow worthy of its instant celebration. Somehow far out to your edge the flickering light all the light. Sudden in its stretch. And. Its stretch out somehow inward to its crux. The long thin line of meeting lights. The lone close celebration in your cold bedroom. The one and same in their celebration. If recognised.

You sent for me?

You missed a celebration.

Oh? What were you celebrating?

Life. Just.

Just?

No. Sudden and instant and – all.

Is it over now? The celebration.

What you see before you.

You? You mean you are, were, celebrating yourself?

Its instant celebration. Stay.

You would like me to celebrate with you? Shall we open this bottle of wine?

Yes.

Now stay with it. Whatever it is don't cancel it out. Please. Just stay with it. However small the ... beginning.

Its only – celebration. And. All its instant recognition. Wait. Such sudden joy its space. Sudden and complete its space. Yes. I think we have progressed. Have we? Have we progressed?

Its only knowledge its meeting space. Its burst of light its meeting place. After all. Such progress to where it is.

To where ... you are?

To where-its-celebration-of-all-it-is.

Yes. Yes!

Only sudden the tiny flicker of white light in the room. And only sudden all the light. Far out to its edge its thin horizon. Merging of all the lights it leaves ongoing. Their recognition.

Yes. Ongoing.

As birth. Smudged into wavering light and leaves ongoing itself. And you are ...?

Its smudge. Itself. Each only. Or both. Or. Their recognition.

I'm afraid really. Of spoiling it with questions. I think we shouldn't. Honestly, we shouldn't. But just let me ask you this.

Are we saying more than we have said before?

More. Or less. No matter. Its split second celebration.

Celebration!

Yes. Let's make the most of it.

Two minutes long up the shaft of light broke off. Although unchanged the instant knowledge lacks staying power. So fickle in its own light. Unfixed in its time. Isolated in its space. What progress except each where it is? So celebration leads to ... its own celebration. Mourning to ... mourning. And here ... the empty bottle of celebration. How apt! Let's celebrate the empty bottle of celebration. Might as well. All celebration an empty bottle. Only. Or this. A full bottle. A full bottle that empties out its own celebration.

And her. Her little points marked off for progress. So what if her progress? Where does such progress go? How release it into space it does not recognise? Space that does not recognise it? How she left you then in your exposed state of almost abandon. Smiling in some strange moment. How went it now? What words? God, how inane now in their silent space. Your only silent space.

And now. Gone her very invention. Enough for invention. And. Enough its goneness for your only silent space.

To what you almost only know. Familiar space in the end. Call it failure ... yet even that. To call it. Unite it with its word. For once and all. But even as it says it changes. Not failure. Another word altogether. Some word that fails to come when needed. Yet still exists. Somewhere apart from this context. In its own space. Or apart from it. Apart and only in itself.

Still. Undefeated in your way your still attempt to synthesise. The unrecognisable with what it does not recognise. Such synthesis there. And. Settle in some space of split second between. Just found the edge of such split second you almost knew. Enough for the instant it pervades.

But not enough.

Eavan Boland

The Black Lace Fan My Mother Gave Me

It was the first gift he ever gave her,
buying it for five francs in the Galeries
in prewar Paris. It was stifling.
A starless drought made the nights stormy.

They stayed in the city for the summer.
They met in cafés. She was always early.
He was late. That evening he was later.
They wrapped the fan. He looked at his watch.

She looked down the Boulevard des Capucines.
She ordered more coffee. She stood up.
The streets were emptying. The heat was killing.
She thought the distance smelled of rain and lightning.

These are wild roses, appliquéd on silk by hand,
darkly picked, stitched boldly, quickly.
The rest is tortoiseshell and has the reticent,
clear patience of its element. It is

a worn-out, underwater bullion and it keeps,
even now, an inference of its violation.
The lace is overcast as if the weather
it opened for and offset had entered it.

The past is an empty café terrace.
An airless dusk before thunder. A man running.
And no way now to know what happened then —
none at all — unless, of course, you improvise:

The blackbird on this first sultry morning,
in summer, finding buds, worms, fruit,
feels the heat. Suddenly she puts out her wing —
the whole, full, flirtatious span of it.

The River

You brought me
  to the mouth of a river
in mid-October
  when the swamp maples
were saw-toothed and blemished.
  I remember

how strange it felt —
  not having any
names for the red oak
  and the rail
and the slantways plunge
  of the osprey.

What we said was less
  than what we saw.
What we saw was
  a duck boat, slowly
passing us, a hunter and
  his spaniel and

his gun poised,
  and, in the distance,
the tips of the wild
  rice drowning in
that blue which raids and
  excludes light.

The Shadow Doll

(This was sent to the bride-to-be in Victorian times, by her dressmaker.
It consisted in a porcelain doll, under a dome of glass, modelling the
proposed wedding dress.)

They stitched blooms from ivory tulle
to hem the oyster gleam of the veil.
They made hoops for the crinoline.

Now, in summary and neatly sewn —
a porcelain bride in an airless glamour —
the shadow doll survives its occasion.

Under glass, under wraps, it stays
even now, after all, discreet about
visits, fevers, quickenings and lusts

and just how, when she looked at
the shell-tone spray of seed pearls,
the bisque features, she could see herself

inside it all, holding less than real
stephanotis, rose petals, never feeling
satin rise and fall with the vows

I kept repeating on the night before —
astray among the cards and wedding gifts —
the coffee pots and the clocks and

the battered tan case full of cotton
lace and tissue paper, pressing down, then
pressing down again. And then, locks.

Nuala Ní Dhomhnaill

Chomh Leochailleach Le Sliogán

Chomh leochailleach le sliogán
a caitheadh suas ar chladach
seasaim lasmuigh ded' dhoras
san iarnóin.
Clingeann an clog i bhfad istigh
go neamheaglach
is baineann macalla as na seomraí folmha
im' chomhair.

Istigh sa chistin tá raidió
ag stealladh phopcheoil
is músclaíonn spré beag dóchais
istigh im' bhráid
ach nuair a chuimhním arís air
is cleas é seo i gcoinne robálaithe
agus is fada fuar folamh an feitheamh agam
gan truist do choiscéime ar an bhfód.

Clingim arís
is éiríonn fuaim mhacallach
trés na seomraí arda,
suas an staighre cláir.
Aithním trí pholl na litreach
ar na toisí Seoirseacha
struchtúir laitíse an chriostail
a cheileann nó a nochtann Dia.

Tá rós dearg i gcróca
ar bhord sa halla.
Tá geansaí ag crochadh
leis an mbalustráid.
Tá litreacha oscailte ina lúi timpeall
ar an urlár go neafaiseach.
I mball ar bith
níl blas ná rian díot le fáil.

Istigh sa seomra suite
ar an gclabhar
tá cárta poist a tháinig chughat aniar
ó do ghrá geal. Maíonn sí
gurb é seo an chéad post nó litir
a gheobhair id' thigh nua.
Is air tá radharc gnáthúil turasóireachta
de Bhrú na Bóinne.

Tagairt é seo a thuigeann tú
gan amhras
don "hieros gamos",
an pósadh a deineadh ar Neamh.
Is lasmuigh de chiorcal
teolaí bhur lánúnachais
tá fuar agam fanacht sa doras
i mo dhílleachtaí, i mo spreas.

Tá oighear á sheideadh
trí phóirsí fada gaofaire
sa phabhailiún
is íochtaraí i mo lár.
Tá na seolphíobáin mothála
reoite ina stangadh.
Tá tonnbhualadh mo chroí
mar fharraigí aduain.

Is mo léan mo cheann mailéid,
mo chloigeann peirce,
os comhair an dorais iata seo
cad leis a bhfuil mo shúil?
Nuair a chlingeann an clog
ar chuma an Aingil Mhuire
ab ann a cheapaim go n-osclóidh na Flaithis
is go dtuirlingeoidh orm colúr?

Mar is istigh sa síce amháin
a tharlaíonn míorúiltí
an cheana, an mhathúnachais
is an ghrá,
mar is i dtaibhrithe amháin
a bhíonn an ghrian is an ré ag soilsiú
le chéile is spéir na maidne
orthu araon ag láú

As Fragile As A Shell

As fragile as a shell/thrown up on a rocky foreshore/I stand outside your door/ in the afternoon/The bell rings far inside/stridently/and brings an echo from/the long empty rooms.

In the kitchen the radio/is belting out pop-music/and for a moment/a small gleam of hope/wakes in my chest/but then the more I think of it/I realise that it is a ploy against housebreaking/and there is a long and fruitless wait before me/without the sound of your footstep in this place.

I ring again/and the echoing sound/rises up through the high-ceilinged rooms/and the wooden stairs/Peeping through the letterbox/I recognise in the Georgian proportions/the lattice-structure of a crystal/that both reveals and witholds God.

There's a red rose in a vase/on the hall-table/There's a jumper hanging from the bannister pole./There are opened letters lying about on the floor/nonchalantly/but nowhere/is there a single sign of you to be seen.

Inside in the livingroom/on the mantelpiece/is a postcard come to you/from your lover. She boasts/that this is the first letter or bit of post/you will get in your new house/On it is an ordinary tourist view/of the tumulus at Newgrange.

This is a reference/not lost on you, of course/to the "hieros gamos",/the marriage made in heaven/Outside the warm circle/of your relationship/I stand in the doorway/a worthless person, a motherless child.

An icy wind blows/through the cold porches /of the farthest pavilions/in the depths of my soul./The conduits of emotion are all frozen solid./My heart beats wildly/like strange and treacherous seas.

And damn my wooden head/my feather-brain, what do I expect/waiting here outside the closed door?/When the bell rings inside/for all the world like the bell of the Angelus/do I really expect the sky to open/and a dove to descend upon me from above?

Because it is only inwardly, in the psyche/that miracles happen/of affection, forgiveness/and love/It is only in dreams/that the sun and the moon shine together/in the sky brightly/while the day dawns on them both.

(Trans. Nuala Ní Dhomhnaill)

Gan Do Chuid Éadaigh

Is fearr liom tú
gan do chuid éadaigh ort —
do léine shíoda
is do charabhat,
do scáth fearthainne faoi t'ascaill
is do chulaith
trí phíosa faiseanta
le barr feabhais táilliúrachta,

do bhróga ar a mbíonn
i gcónaí snas,
do láimhinní craiceann eilite
ar do bhois,
do hata crombie
feirchte ar fhaobhar na cluaise —
ní chuireann siad aon ruainne
le do thuairisc.

Mar thíos fúthu,
i ngan fhios don slua
tá corp gan mhaisle, mháchaill
ná míbhua,
lúfaireacht ainmhí allta,
cat mór a bhíonn amuigh
san oíche
is a fhágann sceimhle ina mharbhshruth.

Do ghuailne leathan fairsing
is do thaobh
chomh slím le sneachta séidte
ar an sliabh;
do dhrom, do bhásta singil
is i do ghabhal
an rúta
go bhfuil barr pléisiúrtha ann.

Do chraiceann atá chomh dorcha
is slím
le síoda go mbeadh tiumhas bheilbhite
ina shníomh
is é ar chumhracht airgid luachra
nó meadhg na habhann
go ndeirtear faoi
go bhfuil suathadh fear is ban ann

Mar sin is dá bhrí sin
is tú ag rince liom anocht,
cé go mb'fhearr liom tú
gan do chuid éadaigh ort,
b'fhéidir nárbh aon díobháil duit
gléasadh anois ar an dtoirt
in ionad leath ban Éireann
a mhilleadh is a lot.

Without Your Clothes

Though I much prefer you/minus your clothes/- your silk
shirt/and your tie/your umbrella tucked under the oxter/and
your three-piece suit/tailored in sartorial elegance.

your shoes which always sport/a high shine/your doe-skin
gloves/on your hands/your crombie hat/tipped elegantly over
the ear —/none of them add/a single whit to your presence.

For underneath them/unbeknownst to all/is a peerless
body/without blemish or fault/the litheness of a wild animal/a
great nocturnal cat/prowling and leaving destruction/in its
wake.

Your broad strong shoulders/and your skin/as smooth as
windblown snow/on the mountainside/your back, your
slender waist/and in your crotch/that growing root/that is
pleasure's very source.

Your complexion so dark/and soft/as silk with the pile of
velvet/in its weave/and smelling very much of
meadowsweet/or watermead, as it is called/that they say has
power/to lead men and women astray.

Therefore, and for that reason/when you go dancing with me
tonight/though I would prefer you stark naked/by my side/I
suppose you had better/put your clothes on/rather than have
half the women of Ireland/totally undone.

(Trans. Nuala Ní Dhomhnaill)

Cailleach

Taibhríodh dom gur mé an talamh
gur mé paróiste Fionntrá
ar a fhaid is ar a leithead,
soir, siar, faoi mar a shíneann sí.
Gurb é grua na Maoilinne grua
mo chinn agus Sliabh an Iolair
mo chliathán aniar;
gurb iad leaca na gcnoc
mo lorgain is slat
mo dhroma is go raibh an fharraige
ag líric mo dhá throigh
ag dhá charraig sin na Páirce,
Rinn Dá Bhárc na Fiannaíochta.

Bhí an taibhreamh chomh beo
nuair a dhúisíos ar maidin
gur fhéachas síos féachaint an raibh,
de sheans, mo dhá chois fliuch.
Ansan d'imíos is dhearmhadas
a raibh tárlaithe, ó,
tá dhá bhliain is breis
anois ann, déarfainn
go dtí le fíordhéanaí
gur cuireadh i gcuimhne arís dom
fuíoll mo thromluí
de bharr líonrith m'iníne.

Bhíomair thíos ar an dtráigh
is bhí sí traochta.
Do chas sí abhaile
ach do leanas-sa orm ag siúl romham.
Ní fada gur chuala í
ag teacht chugham agus saothar uirthi,
í ag pusáil ghoil le teann coisíochta.
"Cad tá ort?". "Ó, a Mhaim, táim sceimhlithe.
Tuigeadh dom go raibh na cnoic ag bogadaíl,
gur fathach mná a bhí ag luascadh a cíocha,
is go n-eireódh sí aniar agus mise d'íosfadh."

The Hag

I dreamed once that I was the land/the Parish of Ventry/in it
length and breadth/That the brow of the Maoileann/was the
brow of my head and Mount Eagle/the side of my chest/the
base of the hillside/my thighs and backbone/and that the sea
was lapping/ my two feet/the two great pocks òf Parkmore
Point/Rinn Dá Bhárc of the Fenian tales.

The dream was so vivid/when I woke up in the morning/
couldn't help bending down to see/if, by any chance, my feet
were wet/Then I went off and forgot/all that had happened/oh
a good two years ago it is now/I'd say/ until very recently/my
daughter's fright/brought back to me/the residue of my
nightmare.

We were down on the strand and she was tired/She turned
home/but I was determined to walk on alone/Before I had got
far/I heard her running back to me, breathlessly/snivelling and
sobbing between the steps/"What's wrong?" "Oh Mom, I'm
terrified/I thought I saw the hills were moving/like a giantess
with swaying breasts/and that she was about to arise and
gobble me up."

(Trans. Nuala Ní Dhomhnaill)

Contributors' Notes

LINDA ANDERSON comes from Belfast and now lives in London. She has published two highly acclaimed novels, *To Stay Alive* (Bodley Head, 1984) and *Cuckoo* (Bodley Head, 1986, Brandon Press, 1988). Her stories and poetry have appeared in various collections including *Pillars of the House: An Anthology of Irish Women's Poetry* (Wolfhound Press, 1987), *Women on War* (Simon and Schuster, 1988) and *Storia* (Pandora Press, 1988). *Charmed Lives*, her first play, won a prize in the London Writer's Competition 1988. She has recently been writer-in-residence at Trent Polytechnic, Nottingham.

LELAND BARDWELL grew up in Leixlip, County Kildare. Left home to seek her fortune, lived in London and Paris during the late 40s and 50s. Returned to Dublin in 1960. Has two daughters and one son living in England, three sons living in Dublin. Now lives in County Monaghan. Writes plays, fiction, poetry. Her plays have been produced on stage and radio and her work has appeared in numerous literary magazines. Has published two volumes of poetry: *The Mad Cyclist* (New Writers Press, 1970) and *The Fly and the Bed Bug* (Beaver Row Press, 1984). Her first collection of short stories, *Different Kinds of Love*, was published by Attic Press in 1987 and her novels include *Girl on a Bicycle* (1978), *That London Winter*, (1981), and *The House* (1984), all published by Co/Op Books. Her latest novel, *There We Have Been*, was published by Attic Press in 1989.

MARY BECKETT taught in Ardoyne, Belfast, until 1956 when she moved to Dublin with her husband. She began writing short stories at the age of twenty-three for BBC radio and then for literary magazines. She stopped writing for twenty years while rearing two daughters and three sons. She has published two novels, *A Belfast Woman* (Poolbeg Press, 1980, William Morrow, 1989), and *Give Them Stones* (Bloomsbury, 1987, Beech Tree Books, 1988) and is at present completing her first collection of short stories.

SARA BERKELEY was born in Dublin in 1967, and is a final-year English student at Trinity College, Dublin. While still at school she won prizes in the Irish Schools Creative Writing Awards and her poems were published in newspapers and in several Raven Arts Press anthologies, including *Raven Introductions 3*. Her first collection, *Penn*, was published in 1986 and the second, *Home Movie Nights*, in 1989, both by Raven Arts Press. She is spending a year on a scholarship to the University of California at Berkeley in 1989-90.

MAEVE BINCHY taught History and French in Dublin before joining *The Irish Times* as a columnist - a position she still holds. She lives in London with her husband, the writer Gordon Snell. She has written four plays, produced on stage and television, and has published five collections of short stories: *Central Line, Victoria Line, The Lilac Bus, Dublin 4*, and *Silver Wedding*.Her best-selling novels are *Light a Penny Candle*, (Century, 1984), *Echoes* (Century, 1985), and *Firefly Summer* (Century, 1987).

EAVAN BOLAND lives in Dublin with her husband Kevin Casey and two daughters. Her collections of poetry include *New Territory* (1967), *The War Horse* (1975), *In Her Own Image* (1980), *Night Feed* (1982), *The Journey* (1986), all published by Arlen House. Her *Selected Poems* was published in 1989 by Carcanet Press and her next collection, *Outside History*, will be published later this year.

DEIRDRE BRENNAN was born in Dublin in 1934. Spent her youth in County Tipperary, studied for her BA in English and Latin at University College Dublin and now lectures at St Patrick's College, Carlow. She writes bilingually. Her first collection of poems in Irish, *I Reilig Na mBan Rialta* was published by Coiscéim in 1974 and the second, *Scothanna Geala*, which appeared in 1989 is Poetry Ireland's book choice of the year.

MOYA CANNON was born in Donegal and now lives in Galway, where she teaches in a school for travelling children. Over the past ten years her work has appeared in many Irish and International poetry journals. Some of her poems have been set to music by the Galway-based composer, Jane O'Leary. Her first collection, *The Foot of Muckish*, will be published in 1989.

EVELYN CONLON was born in Monaghan in 1952. She travelled for a number of years in Australia and Asia, and now

Movement since the early 70s, she was a founder member of the Dublin Rape Crisis Centre and counts starting a crèche in Maynooth College as her most important political activity. Her fiction, poetry and criticism have appeared in numerous journals and anthologies including *Midland Review* (1986), *Graph* (1988), *Ms Muffet and Others* (Attic Press, 1986), and *In Other Words* (Hutchinson, 1987). Her first collection of short stories, *My Head is Opening*, was published by Attic Press in 1987, who also published her first novel, *Stars in the Daytime*, in 1989.

ROZ COWMAN was born in Cork, grew up in Clonmel and lived in East and West Africa for several years. She now lives in County Waterford where she teaches in Adult Education. She has two daughters and one son. Her poems and reviews have appeared in various literary magazines and anthologies including *The Salmon, Irish Review, Poetry Ireland, Midland Review, Oxford Poetry, Rubicon, The Women's Review of Books, Arlen House Anthology 3* (1982), *Raven Introductions* (1984). In 1985 she won the Patrick Kavanagh Award for her poetry.

EILÉAN Ní CHUILLEANÁIN was educated in Cork and, briefly, at Oxford, and is Lecturer in Medieval and Renaissance English at Trinity College, Dublin. She and her husband, the poet Macdara Woods, have one son, Niall. A co-founder/editor of *Cyphers* since 1975, her poetry has been widely published both in Ireland and abroad. Her first collection, *Acts and Monuments*, (Gallery Books, 1972) won the Patrick Kavanagh Award. Three further collections have also been published by Gallery Books: *Site of Ambush* (1975), *Cork* (1977) and *The Rose Geranium* (1981). Her selected poems, *The Second Voyage* (Gallery Books), appeared in 1977 and was reissued, with revisions, in 1981 (Wake Forest University Press). In 1985 she edited and contributed to an anthology of essays, *Irish Women: Image and Achievement* (Arlen House). Her new collection of poems will be published in 1989.

NUALA Ní DHOMHNAILL is a middle-class, middle-aged mother of three who insists on writing in Irish only, for perfectly good political and feminist reasons (think a little about it!). A sincere conviction that poetry can change the world and that women's poetry *en masse* is about to do just that. Her work has appeared in many periodicals and in anthologies such as *Pillars of the House* (Wolfhound Press,1987), *The Other Voice - Twentieth Century Women's Poetry in Translation* (Norton, 1976), *Contemporary Irish Poetry* (University of California Press, 1988),

An Tonn gheal/The Bright Wave (Raven Arts, 1986). She has published two collections of poetry, *An Dealg Droighinn* (Cló Mercier, 1981) and *Fear Suaithinseach* (An Sagart, 1984). Her *Selected Poems* (trans. Michael Hartnett) was published by Raven Arts in 1986, followed by a dual language edition in 1988. She has written plays for both children and adults and the Abbey Theatre will shortly stage *Mo Theaghled*.

MARY DORCEY was born and brought up in Dublin. She has travelled widely and has lived in France, England, America and Japan. Active in the Women's Movement since the 70s, she began to write in the early 80s. She has given many readings of her work in Ireland, Britain and Europe, and her poetry and stories have been published in numerous magazines and in anthologies such as *Girls Next Door* (*The* Women's Press, 1985), *Bread and Roses* (Virago, 1984), *Naming the Waves* (Virago, 1988), *Mad and Bad Fairies* (Attic Press, 1987), *New Angles* (Oxford University Press, 1987), *Beautiful Barbarians* (1986), *Pied Piper* (1989). Her first collection of poems, *Kindling*, appeared in 1982, and she has just completed a second volume, *Not Everyone sees this Night*, all published by Onlywomen Press. Her first collection of stories, *A Noise From the Woodshed* will also be published by Onlywomen Press in 1989. She is now living in County Kerry, and working on a novel.

ÉILÍS Ní DHUIBHNE was born in Dublin in 1954 and educated at Scoil Caitríona and University College Dublin where she won a scholarship to Denmark in 1978 to study Danish and Folklore at the University of Denmark. She was awarded a PhD on Irish folklore in 1982 and since then she has worked as a keeper in the National Library of Ireland and as a lecturer in Folklore. Her first story was published in *The Irish Press* in 1974. Her stories, poems and articles have since appeared in various periodicals, magazines and anthologies including *Best Short Stories 1986* (Heinemann). She was awarded an Arts Council Bursary in literature in 1987. Her first collection of short stories, *Blood and Water*, was published in 1988 by Attic Press, who will also publish her novel, *The Bray House*, in 1990.

ÁINE Ní GHLINN was born in County Tipperary and now lives in Dublin where she works as a presenter/reporter on RTE's Irish language TV programme "Cursaí". Her work has appeared in various Irish and English language magazines and in anthologies such as *An Fhiliocht Chomhaimseartha* (Coiscéim, 1987) and *Pillars of the House* (Wolfhound Press, 1987). *An Chéim*

Bhriste, her first collection of poems, was published in 1984 by Coiscéim. Her second collection, *Gairdín Pharthais agus dánta eile* (Coiscéim, 1988) was awarded Duais Bhord na Gaeilge at Listowel Writers Week in 1987, and 'Ospidéal', one of the poems from the collection, won an Oireachtas award in 1985.

ANNE LE MARQUAND HARTIGAN. Although reared and educated in England, she has lived in Ireland, Louth and Dublin, since 1962. She has been married, has six children and has reared hens without losing one chick! A dramatist as well as a poet, her play, *Beds,* was performed at the Dublin Theatre Festival in 1982 and her epic poem, *Now is a Moveable Feast,* was produced on RTE in 1981. As a painter, her last one woman show was in Dublin at the Temple Bar Gallery in 1985. She has won awards for her poetry and also for her work in Batik. She has given many readings of her poetry both in Ireland and abroad, has been an active member of UCD Women's Studies Forum and is a member of WAAG (Women Artists Action Group). Her work has appeared in various anthologies including *Contemporary Irish Poetry* (1988), *Pillars of the House* (Wolfhound Press, 1987), *Poets Aloud Abu* (1988), *Sleeping with Monsters* (1989), *Sweeping Beauties* (Attic Press, 1989), *Irish Women's Short Stories* (Beacon Press, forthcoming). Her two collections of poems are *Long Tongue* (1982) and *Return Single* (1986), published by Beaver Row Press.

RITA ANN HIGGINS was born in Galway. She left school at an early age and developed an interest in reaching age twenty-two when recuperating from tuberculosis. She started writing in 1982, and her first collection of poems, *Goddess on the Mervue Bus,* was published by Salmon Publishing in 1986. She was awarded an Arts Council writing bursary in the same year and was writer-in-residence in Galway Library in 1987. Her collection, *Witch in the Bushes* (Salmon Publishing), appeared in 1988. She has read on radio and television and has had her work performed by Galway Theatre Workshop and on television.

BIDDY JENKINSON has had her work published in *Comhar, Feasta, Innti,* and *Poetry Ireland* and in *Pillars of the House* (Wolfhound Press, 1987). Coiscéim published both her collections of poetry: *Baisteach Gintli* (1986) and *Uisci Beatha* (1988).

MAEVE KELLY grew up in Dundalk, County Louth. She qualified in General Nursing in London and did postgraduate theatre nursing in Oxford. With her husband, she farmed for many years in County Clare. They now live in Limerick and have a son and a daughter. She is a founding member of the Limerick Federation of Women's Organisations and a founder of *Adapt*, the Limerick Centre for Abused Women and their children, of which she is Administrator. She runs writing workshops from time to time. Her writing has appeared in a wide range of anthologies and magazines including *The Bodley Head Book of Short Stories* (Bodley Head, 1980), *Best Irish Short Stories* (Paul Elek, 1977), *Modern Irish Short Stories* (*Irish Times*, 1985), *Midland Review* (1986) and in *Ms Muffet and Others* (1986), *Mad and Bad Fairies* (1987) and *Sweeping Beauties* (1989), all published by Attic Press.. She has published a collection of short stories, *A Life of Her Own* (Poolbeg Press, 1976), a poetry collection, *Resolution* (Blackstaff, 1986) and a novel, *Necessary Treasons* (Michael Joseph, 1985). Her second novel, *Florrie's Girls*, will be published by Michael Joseph in 1989.

RITA KELLY was born in Galway and now lives in County Wexford. She writes fiction, poetry, criticism and drama. She has received various literary awards, including an Arts Council bursary. Her work, which has been translated into German, Dutch and Italian, has been broadcast on radio and television and published in numerous Irish and international magazines and journals. Her poems and fiction have appeared in a number of anthologies including *A Dream Recurring and Other Stories* (Arlen House,1980), *Modern Irish Short Stories* (*Irish Times*, 1985), *An Fhilíocht Chomhaimseartha* (Coiscéim, 1987). Her first collection of short stories, *The Whispering Arch and Other Stories*, was published by Arlen House in 1986. *Dialann sa Díseart* (with Eoghan Ó Tuairisc) (Coiscéim) appeared in 1981 and *An Bealach Eadoigh* (Coiscéim) in 1984.

MEDBH MCGUCKIAN was born in Belfast and studied English at Queen's University. In 1979 she won the British National Poetry Competition, which led to her first book. She has three sons, has worked as a teacher and as writer-in-residence at Queen's. Currently, she is Literary Editor of the Belfast magazine, *Fortnight*. In 1980 she published two pamphlets, *Single Ladies* (Interim Press) and *Portrait of Joanna* (Ulsterman Press). Her three collections have been published by Oxford University Press: *The Flower Master* (1982), *Venus and the Rain* (1984) and *On Ballycastle Beach* (1988). Her work has appeared in many magazines and in the *Penguin Book of Contemporary British Verse* (1983) and the *Faber Book of Contemporary Irish Verse* (1985).

MÁIRE MHAC an tSAOI was born in Dublin in 1922, and was educated at Alexandra School and at University College Dublin. She was called to the Bar in 1944 and obtained an MA in classical modern Irish in 1945. She joined the Department of Foreign Affairs and served in Paris and Madrid, and as Irish representative to the Council of Europe. She and her husband Conor Cruise O'Brien have two adopted children. She is currently visiting lecturer in the Department of Folklore and Folklife at the University of Pennsylvania, USA. Her collections of poetry include *Margabh na Saoire* (1956), *A Heart Full of Thought* (translations from the Irish) (1959), *Codladh an Ghaiscigh* (1973), *An Galan Dubhach* (1980), *An Cion Go Dtí Seo* (Sairséal Ó Marcaigh, 1987). She has published articles, short stories, essays and translations in various newspapers and periodicals.

GERARDINE MEANEY was born in Waterford in 1962 and educated in Kilkenny and at University College Dublin. She is a feminist critic and is currently Junior Research Fellow in the Institute of Irish Studies, Queen's University, Belfast, where she is working on the fiction of Kate O'Brien. In 1986 she won a Hennessy Award for New Irish Writing. Her stories have appeared in newspapers and in journals and in the *Midland Review* (1986) special issue on Irish women's writing.

PAULA MEEHAN studied at Trinity College Dublin and Eastern Washington University. She has published two collections of poetry, *Return and No Blame* (1984) and *Reading the Sky* (1986), both from Beaver Row Press. Her poems have been broadcast on radio and television, and have appeared in many Irish and international magazines. Her work has been included in *Pillars of the House* (Wolfhound Press, 1987) and the *Midland Review* (1986).

FRANCES MOLLOY was born in Derry. Mother of two. Lived in Lancashire for eighteen years, but came back to Ireland to live and work in 1988. Currently of no fixed abode. Much worn out by many flittings. Grateful to countless friends for their kindnesses. Worries that someone might tip the pope off regarding her outrageous blasphemies. Has had many short stories published in various magazines and anthologies. Highly acclaimed first novel, *No Mate for the Magpie* (Virago Press, 1985). Currently completing second novel commissioned by Virago, and tying up a volume of short stories.

CLAIRR O'CONNOR was born in Limerick and educated there and at University College Cork and St. Patrick's College Maynooth. She is married to Kevin Honan, has one son, and works as a teacher. She has had poems and stories published in numerous Irish, English and American journals and anthologies. Her play, *Getting Ahead*, was broadcast on BBC Radio 4. In 1988 she was Irish Exchange writer at New Dramatists in New York, where her plays, *No Return* and *House of Correction*, were given staged readings. Her first collection of poems, *When You Need Them*, was published by Salmon Publishing in 1989.

MARY E O'DONNELL was born in Monaghan in 1954, and now lives in Maynooth, County Kildare. Her poems and short stories have been published in *New Irish Writing*, *Poetry Ireland Review*, *The Irish Times*, *Cyphers*, *Krino*, *Orbis*, *Oxford Poetry* and other periodicals and magazines. Her work has been anthologised in *Midland Review* and *Pillars of the House* (Wolfhound Press, 1987). She has won many prizes and awards for her poetry, and given numerous readings and radio/TV broadcasts. She works as a theatre critic for *The Sunday Tribune*.

EITHNE STRONG was born in West Limerick and came to work in Dublin in 1942. That year her first published poetry - in Irish - appeared in *An Glór*. In 1943 she was a founder member of the Runa Press, a struggling outlet for many poets. She then had nine children, the youngest mentally handicapped. She combined family care with writing, taking a degree in Trinity College, Dublin and teaching for twelve years. Writing in both Irish and English, her work has appeared in many magazines, journals and anthologies published in Ireland and abroad, has been broadcast on radio, and translated into French and Italian. Her first novel, *Degrees of Kindred*, (Tansy Books), came out in 1979, followed by a collection of short stories, *Patterns* (Poolbeg Press, 1981). Her collections of poetry include *Songs of Living* (Runa Press, 1961), *Sarah, in Passing* (Dolmen Press, 1974), *Flesh - The Greatest Sin*, (Runa Press, 1980), *Cirt Oibre* (Coiscéim, 1980), *Fuil agus Fallai* (Coiscéim, 1983), *My Darling Neighbour* (Beaver Row Press, 1985).

DOLORES WALSHE was educated at University College and at Trinity College in Dublin. Has lived and worked in Dublin, Belfast, New York, Amsterdam and San Rafael, California, with a wide range of nationalities. Has translated Dutch film scripts for UNICEF in Holland and trained as a suicide counsellor in California. In 1987 she obtained first place in the OZ Whitehead/Society of Irish Playwrights/PEN Literary award, was short-listed for the Hennessy Literary Award and was also an award-winner in *The Sunday Tribune*/Powers short story competition. Her prize-winning play, *In the Talking Dark*, was staged by the Royal Exchange Theatre, Manchester, in 1989. Her poetry and short stories have appeared in newspapers, magazines and anthologies.

UNA WOODS was born and brought up in Belfast and later spent some years in the South of England and in Dublin. She is now living in Belfast with her husband and two children. Her poetry and short stories have appeared in various magazines and anthologies including *The Female Line* (Northern Ireland Women's Rights Movement, 1985) and *The Blackstaff Book of Short Stories* (Blackstaff Press, 1988). Her first book, *The Dark Hole Days*, a novella and short stories, was published by Blackstaff Press in 1984.

Bibliography

ARCHER, Nuala (Ed). Feature Issue *'Contemporary Irish Women's Writing'*. USA: Midland Review 3, 1986

BOLAND, Eavan. *'The Woman Poet: Her Dilemma'*. USA: Midland Review 3, 1986

BOLAND, Eavan. *A Kind of Scar: The Woman Poet in a National Tradition*. Dublin: Attic Press, LIP pamphlet 1989

BOOKS IRELAND. *'Irish Women's Writing'*. Dublin: Books Ireland, Special Issue March, 1988

BYRON, Catherine. *'A House of One's Own: Three Contemporary Women Poets'*. UK: Women's Review 19, 1987

CONLON, Evelyn. *'Millions Like us — Women in Irish Literary Culture'*. Dublin: Graph 5, 1988

HARGREAVES, Tamsin. *'Feeling in the Short Stories of Mary Lavin'*. Dublin: Studies 76 (303), 1987

HARTIGAN, Anne Le Marquand. *The Mute Voice, The Deaf Ear*. Dublin: UCD Women's Studies Forum Working Papers, 1987

HOOLEY, Ruth (Ed). *The Female Line: Northern Irish Women Writers (Anthology)*. Belfast: Northern Ireland Women's Rights Movement, 1985

JOHNSON, Toni O'Brien. *'Questions for Irish Feminist Criticism'* UK: Text and Context 3, 1988

KANE, Marie. *'Maeve Kelly and New Irish Women Writing'*. UK/USA: Women's Studies International Forum 5 (5), 1982.

KELLY, AA (Ed). *Pillars of the House: An Anthology of Verse by Irish Women from 1690 to the Present*. Dublin: Wolfhound, 1987

KILFEATHER, Siobhan. *Beyond the Pale: Sexual Identity and National Identity in Early Irish Fiction*. USA: Princeton, Critical Matrix Working Papers, 1986

KLEAR Writer's Group. *Notions: A Collection of Short Stories and Poems*. Dublin: KLEAR/Borderline Publications, 1987

Nic DHIARMADA, Briona. *'Tradition and the Female Voice in Contemporary Poetry in Irish'*. Attic Press/Women's Studies International Forum II (4), 1988

Ní DHOMHNAILL, Nuala. *'Making the Millennium: Nuala Ní Dhomhnaill in conversation with Michael Cronin'*. Dublin: Graph 1, 1986

McELROY, James. *'Night Feed: An Overview of Ireland's Women Poets'*. USA: The American Poetry Review, February, 1985

McKAY, Susan. *'A Literature of Our Own. Recent Fiction by Irish Women'*. Belfast: Linen Hall Review 1 (1), 1984

MEANEY, Gerardine. *'History Gasps: Myth in the Poetry of Eiléan Ní Chuilleanáin and Sara Berkeley'*. UK: Studies in Contemporary Irish Literature Vol.2, Forthcoming.

MONAGHAN, Patricia (Ed). *Unlacing: Irish—American Women Poets (Anthology)*. Fairbanks: Fireweed Press, 1987

NÍ CHUILLEANÁIN, Eiléan. *'Women as Writers: Dánta Grá to Maria Edgeworth, in Irish Women — Image and Achievement*, Eiléan Ní Chuilleanáin (Ed.) Dublin: Arlen House, 1985

NÍ CHUILLEANÁIN, Eiléan. *Woman as Writer: The Social Matrix*. Dublin: Crane Bag 4 (1), 1980

O'DONOVAN, Katie. *Irish Women Writers (Pamphlet)*. Dublin: Raven Arts Press, 1988

O'FAOLAIN, Nuala. *'Irish Women and Writing in Modern Ireland'* in *Irish Women Image and Achievement*. Dublin: Arlen House, 1985

QUINN, John. *Portrait of the Artist as a Young Girl (Eavan Boland, Maeve Binchy, Claire Boylan, Polly Devlin, Jennifer Johnston, Molly Keane, Mary Lavin, Joan Lingard, Dervla Murphy, Edna O'Brien)*. London: Methuen, 1986

SIMPSON, Janet Madden (Ed). *Woman's Part: An Anthology of Short Fiction by and about Women*. Dublin: Arlen House, 1984

SIMPSON, Janet Madden *'Womanwriting: The Art of Textual Politics'* in *Personally Speaking: Women's Thoughts on Women's Issues*. Liz Steiner Scott (Ed). Dublin: Attic Press, 1985

SMYTH, Ailbhe. *'Ireland's Rebel Daughters: Feminist Publishers'* USA: Women's Review of Books 14 (7), 1987

SMYTH, Ailbhe. *'The Floozie in the Jacuzzi: Intersextextual Inserts'*. Cork: The Irish Review 6, 1989

WILLS, Clair. *'The Perfect Mother: Authority in the Poetry of Medbh McGuckian'*. UK: Text and Context 3, 1988